THE HOCKEY WORKSHOP

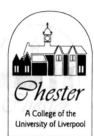

The HOCKEY WORKSHOP

WORKSHOP

A Complete Game Guide

David Whitaker

The Crowood Press

First published in 1992 by
The Crowood Press Ltd
Ramsbury, Marlborough
Wiltshire SN8 2HR

This impression 1997

British Library Cataloguing in Publication Data

A catalogue record for this book is available from the British
Library.

ISBN 1 85223 114 9 (HB)
     1 85223 727 9 (PB)

Acknowledgements
The compilation of this book has taken several years and I am most
grateful to the many players and coaches who have assisted in
extending and deepening my knowledge of hockey, thus
providing me with the raw material for this volume.
    I am particularly grateful to David Faulkner and Russell Garcia
who agreed to appear in the photographs, and Trevor Adams who
produced them; John Hurst, Sue Slocombe and Bernie Cotton who
provided the vast majority for the chapters on Goalkeeping and
Young Players and Management respectively; but most of all to
Chris Whitaker who yet again did so much in the production and
initial editing stage.
    Without any of this support I doubt if I would have completed
the challenge.

Dedication
To Mum and Dad.

Throughout this book the pronouns 'he', 'him' and 'his' have been
used inclusively and are intended to apply to both males and
females.

Picture Credits
The colour photographs were supplied by Allsport; the black and
white sequences were taken by Trevor Adams.
The line-drawings are by Taurus Graphics.

Cover design by Visual Image.
Cover illustrations: colour photographs supplied by Allsport,
black and white photographs by Trevor Adams; line-drawings by
Taurus Graphics.

Typeset by Chippendale Type Ltd., Otley,
West Yorkshire.
Printed in Hong Kong by South China Printing Co.

CONTENTS

Key

left back	LB
right back	RB
left half	LH
centre half	CH
centre forward	CF
inside left	IL
inside right	IR
right wing	RW
left wing	LW
right half	RH

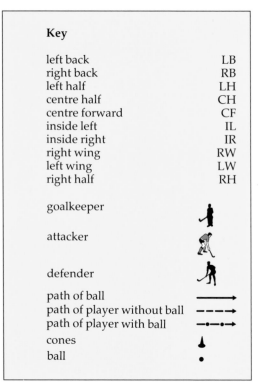

goalkeeper

attacker

defender

path of ball

path of player without ball

path of player with ball

cones

ball

PREFACE

Hockey has undergone a revolution since about 1980. Not only are artificial pitches much more numerous but also a rapidly increasing proportion of all quality hockey is now being played on these surfaces. The greatest benefit of these pitches is that the game is now more a battle of skill than a matter of luck. This emphasis upon skill has attracted more young players into the game.

The nature of artificial turf has increased the physical demands of the game, leading to rapid improvements in the fitness levels of players. At the 1986 World Cup it was shown that most international players were covering between 8,000 and 9,000m during a game. The change in the offside rule to cover only the final attacking quarter of the pitch is likely not only to increase this distance for most players but also to demand a higher intensity performance.

While at club level the distances may be shorter, the increase in both amount and intensity is likely to be similar.

These changes have challenged coaches considerably: more young players want to learn the game; club teams are seeking coaches who will help them aspire to higher standards; clubs are introducing coaching programmes for both the youth and their elite players; and the standards in the game are forever improving.

The principal objectives of this book are to help coaches and players develop their personal abilities in their chosen areas. I hope to be able to share some of my own experiences developed during twenty-five years of involvement in playing and coaching at all levels.

I believe that one of the major resources that any coach has is his own mind – I have therefore tried throughout not just to provide solutions, but to offer principles upon which a decision would be based, so that the reader can draw his own conclusions.

The principal reason for my emphasis upon a problem-solving approach to coaching is that games coaching is riddled with too much direction (or coach-orientated work). Games are in fact dynamic environments demanding recognition and decision-making skills, and we have a responsibility as coaches to develop these skills in players at the earliest opportunity. While clear direction by the coach is necessary, players must be educated in the skill of choosing in order to recognize particular situations, improve their decision-making skills and develop their understanding of the game – all key components in team play.

The problem-solving approach to coaching should complement free exploration and didactic approaches, but is perhaps rather underused. It helps to identify specific problems or challenges while at the same time not imposing the solutions from the very outset; it utilizes the knowledge and experiences of the players within the learning process, with the coach directing the process so that the greatest advances possible can be made both for the individual players concerned and the small group or team involved. This method obviously demands that the coach should have models of the various solutions to the problems so that progress can be directed and assisted. But he must also have an open mind for new solutions or modifications to existing solutions, and be able to assess, adapt and perfect these so that they may be integrated into the play to the greatest advantage of the players.

It is always important to look at both sides of a problem situation. For example, when considering an attacking move, if only the attack is assessed and no evaluation of the aims, objectives and likely movements of the defence is made, then important pointers to the best possible solutions for the attack can easily be missed. It has been known for attackers to think that a certain pattern of movement would be to their advantage, when in fact it was exactly what the defenders would prefer them to do!

One of the most challenging areas of this problem-solving approach is identifying the challenges or areas in which improvement is required. While this is of course a starting point, it is based upon the evaluation of previous performance, emphasizing the interactive nature of planning, monitoring and evaluation of every aspect of play in a sport.

The Hockey Workshop is divided into three parts: The Components, The Workshop and The Support Systems. The first part looks at the players and the coach, the two principal components of the coaching process. The second part details the work that will be done when the coach is working with players; this is the core of coaching. The last section addresses the support systems that are necessary to give players and coaches the opportunity to succeed.

If, through this book, I can help you develop your own abilities so that you can contribute even more to hockey, then I will feel I have truly achieved my goal.

THE COMPONENTS

PART 1

1

THE PLAYERS

Initially, a player should be considered for the things he does well, as these are what he has to offer a team. A player's weaknesses should always be a secondary issue. Some of his perceived weaknesses may, in the game situation, be shown to be irrelevant (e.g. desire to win); others may be covered by roles assigned to other members of the team; while a number may require urgent attention if the player is to fulfil his potential within the team.

Realistically, a coach can very rarely have exactly what he wants and what the team needs in every player, and a compromise is necessary. The skill of coaching is to minimize this compromise.

This chapter will look at the demands of the game, the types of player, the needs of players, the importance of playing roles rather than playing formations and the types of role that exist at individual, group and team level.

The Nature of the Game

This has an important effect upon players, their commitment and contribution to the game.

On artificial turf the nature of the surface results in the ball being in play for longer periods and the players therefore being more active during the 70 minutes. The multiple sprint activity in the game, both with and without the ball, puts considerable demands upon the players. At all levels of play artificial pitches necessitate greater physical effort to maintain a playing standard, and this is reflected in the physiological training expected of players. The rules and techniques of the game put additional stresses upon players in both the physical and technical areas – the small ball and stick width, combined with the obstruction rule, make the technical aspect of the game rather high, while the alteration of the offside law to cover only the attacking quarter increases the physical demands of the game still further.

There are also the psychological stresses found in all team sports, which function not only at the individual level but also the group and team levels. Team sports demand a level of social interaction between members; players must want to be part of a team and also be willing to subjugate their personal needs and desires to those of the team. This aspect is probably the most interesting yet least studied, for the truly successful teams are those in which the players want to play for each other. There is no magic formula to this; it is rather a potpourri of many things – skills, patterns of play, individuals, attitudes, fitness, values, desire, tradition, past experience, expectations, leadership and many more diverse factors. The best coaches and managers will know when the combination of players is just right; if there is a combination that is more likely to succeed then it may well be worthwhile investigating the types of player that exist.

Player Profiles

These are, of course, oversimplified stereotypes that seldom exist as such, but they serve to identify 'types' and help coaches and managers understand players a little more. In reality, of course, most players are a mixture of these 'types' in varying

Fig 1   Richard Dodds, captain of the 1988 Olympic champions, playing for England against India in 1985.

proportions. The profiles are primarily orientated to the physical or psychological attributes of players; within every grouping there will naturally also be players of varying technical and tactical ability which would influence their inclusion in a team or squad.

The Gifted Player

This player believes that what he does is the most important and that the other players must respond to his play, rather than vice versa. Most of his performance is therefore self-centred rather than team orientated. Often the gifted player will have outstanding individual abilities which can bring success to the team, but will be a loner socially.

While this kind of player may thus create difficulties in team coaching, he may also bring attributes such as high standards of performance and expectation which may enhance the strength of the team. The gifted player should never be dismissed solely because he is self-centred, as most competitive performers have an element of this in their character. Rather, the coach should evaluate whether his positive contributions to team success outweigh his negative influences over a period of time. Interestingly, the team itself should cope with this kind of player, until they cease to perform at their highest standards when the player's difficulties will grow in importance and outweigh the benefits.

The Players' Player

This player is almost the opposite to the self-centred player. A typical players' player is rarely seen as outstanding by the spectator; instead he is always working for and responding to his team-mates, putting

11

their needs always before his own. The real accolades for this type of player come from his team who recognize his important contribution to their overall success. Players' players are often characterized by their consistency of performance, high work rates, desire to emphasize 'team' success rather than 'individual' success, and impressive levels of motivation.

Leaders

Every squad or team needs a few leaders and they appear in many forms. Some are calm, clinical performers directing their men accordingly; others have great charisma drawing their players around them, driving them onward and always leading by example; while still others seem to lie dormant and then rise to the occasion giving a sudden extra input of strength and commitment to the team. While there are many types of leader, they all give out similar qualities to their players, though in different ways: they give them confidence to perform, strength to persevere, guidance, discipline, belief, etc.

Strongmen

This is a rather contentious sphere as all too often this kind of description is misconstrued to promote nasty, illegal and/or overphysical play. In any competitive team game there is a need to have a number of players who have very high levels of physical and psychological strength. If possible, the whole team will be like this; inevitably though there will always be a few players who are mentally and physically tougher than the rest and at some time in a tournament or match, their attributes will be called upon to provide an example to the team. This may only be for a few seconds but the influence on the team is remarkable.

In 1976 Southgate were playing Alma Arta (USSR) in the European Club Cup. Southgate were struggling in a titantic battle, with the physical attributes of the Russian club beginning to wear them down. The turning point was when the Alma Arta centre forward turned with the ball and ran straight into Tony Ekins, Southgate's centre half. The Russian, for all his strength and power, came off a clear second best (collapsing to the ground like a rapidly deflating balloon) and the whole team gained in confidence and went on to win.

A second example was at the Los Angeles Olympics during the bronze medal match against Australia, where Great Britain was under enormous pressure, being kept in the match only by some of the bravest goalkeeping from Ian Taylor that anyone had ever seen. A crucial moment in the game came when Norman Hughes beat an Australian twice his size (and speed!) to a ball in midfield which he had no right to win. Ian's desire had been transmitted to other players and was epitomized by Hughes' actions; Great Britain won 3–2.

Players who have these qualities may often be leaders in a team.

Jokers

Every team or squad requires a full range of personalities if it is to draw the best out of its players. The joker/comedian has an important role to play. The vast majority of hockey players at any level play because they enjoy playing, and even at the highest competitive level this is still an important factor. There are times when coaching sessions have to be lightened, spirits have to be lifted or players have to be relaxed, and if there are players capable of doing this at the appropriate times, then they should be encouraged as it is a useful pressure release valve. Experience shows that the most successful teams sensibly combine these attributes; while it would therefore be unwise to use them as a major criterion for selection, it would be equally unwise to ignore them altogether.

The Team

Players make up the team and teams are usually defined by their playing formation, 3–3–3–1–1 or 5–3–2–1. But is this the

Fig 2 'Please could I explain?' Jeff Archibald of New Zealand is unable to persuade de Vecchi to change his mind.

correct starting point? Is it not the roles assigned to playing positions that are the foundation of team building?

Two teams line up playing the same formation, but the roles assigned to players may vary greatly, resulting in the teams playing very differently. A great deal of time and effort is wasted on formations and far too little is given over to the roles of players both at individual and group level. If the players understand their playing roles and are working in harmony with one another, then the team as a whole will be in harmony. These roles are, of course, the result of an amalgamation of the coach's philosophy and the attributes of players. But that is not the only input to the decision-making unit; players themselves have a philosophy of performing worth getting to know. Mutually agreed goals with the coach are always more likely to succeed. Just as there is considerable dialogue between coach and performer relating to strategies which underpin tactical play in an individual sport, so there should be dialogue in team games. Players require leadership but they also need to be involved in role definition.

The following table outlines the basic roles and requirements normally assigned to playing positions. These are, of course, a generalization, but a valid starting point in role definition.

The coach should add to this table any roles that are important for his team and highlight the principal requirements for each role, thus prioritizing the role requirements.

He should also study the preferred positions of his players as in the table below and consider in which attributes they are strong and in which they need development. A third column could be used for other positive attributes, which would be a further asset to the team. It is useful to involve players personally in the compilation of

13

PLAYING ROLE	OFFENSIVE REQUIREMENTS	DEFENSIVE REQUIREMENTS
Sweeper	Accurate short and long passes plus overhead passes. Intelligent and incisive running with and without the ball into attacking area. Ability to read the game. Confidence with the ball.	Tackling of all kinds. Closing down, shadowing, delaying, channelling forwards who break through with the ball. Speed to get across to through ball and cover points of danger. Controlling all kinds of pass under pressure. Calm authority.
Full back	As above.	As above. Working as a pair to mark CF, cover other defenders and close down a forward breaking through with the ball. Building up a sound defensive understanding with CH and WH.
Centre back	As above but the marking responsibilities often restrict offensive moves to a minimum.	Marking and tackling have a high priority. Marking is player to player on CF. He must be fit and strong enough to cover the running of the forward and then make a tackle or interception.
Right half	Passing is a very high priority as RH is an easy position in which to receive the ball but a difficult position from which to distribute. Disguising and performing a wide variety of passes is important. Vision for attacking moves. Ability to beat an opponent and attack as an IF or wing.	Closing down and tackling using sideline as a colleague. Speed on the turn to counter pace of wing. Ability to work with other defenders in order to slow down and stop attacks on his flank and cover points of danger as opposition penetrate on the other flank.
Left half	As above. Also most passes have to be made from left to right and it is vital that the player is skilful at moving the ball and body into the correct position to do this.	

PLAYING ROLE	OFFENSIVE REQUIREMENTS	DEFENSIVE REQUIREMENTS
	The offensive role is usually less demanding and the player must be capable of performing this more defensive role.	As above. Also strength of reverse side tackle and interception.
Right and left half in 3–3–3–1–1	As above, but offensive roles are restricted by their marking responsibilities. The RH is often used as a more attacking player to support the tight marking RM and the much freer CM.	As above but player to player marking dominates.
Centre half	Provides the principal link between defence and attack. Able to play a variety of passes to IFs so that latter can attack quickly. Ability to collect and give passes in complete 360 degree range so as to maintain momentum and/or change the point of attack. Retaining possession is a high priority in this role. Licence to support IFs and ability to attack opposing circle. Excellent poise, control and vision to set up attacks in open play and at restarts.	CH rarely has a specific marking role but the player must be aware of stopping the direct pass to the CF down the centre of the field; the danger of the crossfield pass between the IFs (defending IFs can help with this); the opposing CH/CM pushing forward with ball; channelling an opposing midfield player who is running with the ball; and covering the central area of the defensive circle and marking any opponent free in that area. Closing down, shadowing, channelling without being beaten are important requirements. Ability to recognize danger points in midfield and react accordingly. Positional play is very important as other defenders take their bearings from relative position of CH.
Centre midfield	As above but this role often has greater licence to move out of the central area in order to act as the play maker. This requires more incisive qualities as noted for IF play and a high level of fitness. Offensive duties generally make up the larger proportion of the role.	As above but the role demands closing down, pressurizing and ball winning at danger points in midfield as other defenders (except sweeper) are marking player to player. Against another 3–3–3–1–1 formation, there is often a need to pay close attention to the opposing CM.

PLAYING ROLE	OFFENSIVE REQUIREMENTS	DEFENSIVE REQUIREMENTS
Inside forward	Role of principal play maker in 5–3–2–1 system. Incisive dribbling, a wide variety of skills plus vision and deception are important abilities to link IF with surrounding players. Ability to receive passes from behind and retain possession in the tight confines of midfield. The work-load requires high standards of fitness.	Primary role is to stop the ball getting to the opposing IF by marking alongside or in front of the player rather than behind him. Positioning and interception skills are very important, not only for the IF but also the strikers as they work as a team particularly at restarts. Closing down players in midfield and tackling are also vital qualities.
Left and right midfield	If the emphasis is on marking tightly and winning the ball, the offensive role is limited to the times when the ball is won or the team is dominating. After winning the ball simple, accurate passes are the priority, followed by support running. At restarts the ability to control the ball in the tight confines of midfield is vital as is the creation of space for himself or others if marking is player to player.	This is often the principal role of these players and therefore marking, closing down and tackling qualities are important. Player to player marking is usually expected of these players of the opposition IF or midfield over whole defensive area. If one of these players is to be more attacking than the other then the rest of the defence has to be ready to compensate.
Strikers	Speed is a great asset for any wing or centre forward. Ability to make space if tightly marked, take a pass from behind and go forward, offer a lead to moves, beat defenders on either side, centre the ball accurately, and function in any of the front positions. Scoring goals is a major role of these men and therefore poise and balance in performing a variety of shots along with the aggressive attitude necessary in the cut and thrust in front of goal are important. When tight marking is experienced these men should be capable of making space for colleagues coming from deeper positions.	Tackling back, closing down and pressurizing defenders along with good positioning at restarts can give considerable help to team defence.

Name	Position	Assessment of required attributes		Other positive attributes
		Strengths	In need of development	
Smith	Left half	Defensive skills Speed	Recognizing when to join the attack. Teamwork with LB.	Leadership Penalty corner Striking Aerial passes Tenacity

this data as this enhances the relationship between players and coach. By combining all this information, the coach and player should not only be able to structure a role in harmony with both the players' attributes and the team's needs, but also a developmental plan to improve the player.

The Needs of Players

The basic needs of a player in a team can be summed up very simply: to be an accepted and valued member of the team in both the preparation and performance phases.

When players first come together in a team or squad or enter an existing squad, they bring with them many personal concerns, such as where they will fit in, whether they are good enough and will be accepted, what they will be contributing to the team/squad, and what their role will be.

In order to help overcome these potential difficulties, team building that primarily aims to promote the individual's self-esteem and self-confidence is necessary. Some temporary common goals would also help develop a team identity, which would in turn provide a framework within which the individual's progress could be encouraged and nurtured. This process helps establish a relatively safe environment for the players.

Inevitably, within a squad there will be internal competition for places and positions. This is a natural and necessary process, but if not dealt with appropriately can be destructive. While it is difficult to motivate players to share their knowledge for the overall benefit of the squad when selection is not yet settled, it is none the less important. Players must be convinced that there is a simple cyclical process: individual performance when team-orientated leads to team improvement and this in turn promotes the individual's performance again.

Players learn most rapidly when they are given the opportunity to provide input to the learning environment. Any relevant experience can contribute not only to their own development but also to that of the team, generating enthusiasm, responsibility and commitment, and clarifying their role within the squad.

The way a coach works with his players individually and as a team should be integral to his philosophy of coaching. And within the development of his coaching philosophy, the needs of the players ought to be of high priority. This will be considered in the next chapter.

2
THE COACH

The position of *coach* is a responsible and influential one. The incumbent should never be afraid of this post but always be wary and careful of how he utilizes his power: it is not what the role entails that is fraught with danger, only the way it is performed.

Coaching is a complex role involving many different interacting and sometimes even conflicting duties and responsibilities. The aim of this chapter is to simplify these complexities and help coaches formulate priorities in their work.

Philosophy of the Coach

A coaching philosophy is composed of attitudes and values modified by experience over time, but there is a core element to any coach's philosophy which influences anything he does. A coach's philosophy is 'what the coach is': how he moves, talks, thinks, lives and performs as a person in his sport.

The core element is usually related to the level of importance attached to fundamental factors such as winning, the development of players and enjoyment. As in most aspects of life there has to be a sensible balance, and all coaches should spend some time not only assessing the value they give to each of these factors, but also, and more importantly, relating this to their actual performance in the role of coach. While nearly all coaches do emphasize development and enjoyment, all too often they behave in a way that clearly indicates that winning is the key factor.

Over-emphasis upon winning can blind a coach to positive developments in players, while with further positive feedback and assessment these developments may produce improvement and then winning. There is no doubt that winning can be a catalyst for further development but experience suggests that a coach cannot change a player or team into an instant

Characteristics of the Best Coaches

1. The best coaches endeavour to educate and motivate players to aspire to levels that are even on the frontiers of their own ability. In this way the coaches themselves extend and deepen their knowledge.

2. They are rarely afraid of passing a player on to another coach; they see them as colleagues rather than competitors. No one coach has the monopoly on knowledge.

3. They never want to have players dependent upon them – a player should be educated to be a decision-maker not a performing animal. To demand such control could result in inhibiting the very development the coach seeks to foster.

4. The very best coaches are rarely satisfied with their contribution. What was innovative this year, is commonplace the next. The challenges at all levels are ever changing and ongoing and should primarily be self-motivated by the current progress and performance. When a coach evaluates his performance over a programme and concludes that he is satisfied with the level of achievement and there is little to excite him in future involvement, then it is time to step aside and let someone else take the players onward and upward. There is nothing wrong with stepping aside, the aggravation comes from hanging around!

winning unit: there has to be first some positive development of the individual and/or group. The winning factor should therefore be put into perspective. 'Winning' and all the benefits thereof are always a result of development.

There appears to be great confusion and even mistrust of the term 'enjoyment' in coaching, yet one only has to look at the faces of performers when they have achieved success (and that is not measured just by winning a competition) to recognize it. A smile is the most obvious signal but there are several facial expressions that indicate enjoyment of success at any particular moment in time.

The enjoyment, fun, fulfilment, satisfaction or whatever one wishes to label it is the result of a good and effective performance, and coaches should emphasize this and encourage players to enjoy and take pride in such a performance.

Enjoyment fuels interest; interest fires imagination; imagination leads to exploration; exploration promotes development; development increases enjoyment. If there is credence in this process then enjoyment becomes a crucial factor within the coaching philosophy.

So What Makes a Good Coach?

Probably every person has a slightly different answer to this question, but most can be simplified to the following few areas: knowledge of the sport, desire to improve as a coach and understanding the players.

KNOWLEDGE OF THE SPORT

There is no substitute for an in-depth knowledge of the techniques, strategies and tactics of hockey. A detailed understanding allows the coach to lead players through a learning process thoughtfully and effectively, and help them find solutions to the many challenges that arise during training, so preparing them for the match situation. Only through a thorough understanding of all aspects of the game will credibility and respect be gained from the players.

Coaching Styles

A crucial factor to coaching efficiency is one's choice of coaching style. Generally speaking, there are three styles: authoritative/bossy, submissive/minder and co-operative/advising.

Coaches may conform to one or other style according to their attitudes and values but it is important for all coaches to consider the following:

1. The strengths and weaknesses of each style.
2. The reasons why they lean toward a certain style: Was it a conscious decision or was *their* coach/influential educator like that?
3. Differing styles may suit different situations and the best coaches therefore use a mixture in their coaching styles.

The *authoritative/bossy* coach sees himself as the source of all knowledge; he makes all the decisions while the players listen and obey. The players merely respond to instructions rather than participate in the decision-making.

The *submissive/minder* coach, on the other hand, actively shies away from decision-making, leaving the players to look after themselves. There is almost no attempt to organize and educate and discipline is ignored.

Finally, the *co-operative/advising* coach understands the importance of leadership and discipline, while realizing the advantages of involving the performers in the decision-making. Together they select and work towards certain objectives and goals.

DESIRE TO IMPROVE AS A COACH

Knowledge in itself is not enough; the coach must have the desire to want to use this knowledge to its maximum effect. In any case it is unlikely that you have all the knowledge available and the best coaches are always seeking more information relevant to their sport or the art of coaching. This enthusiasm to improve by itself can have a motivating influence on players, as it is an example they respond to and emulate.

UNDERSTANDING THE PLAYERS

This is often viewed with scepticism by some coaches who believe that players are there to perform and to do what they are told by the coach. This rather dictatorial style is not one that will draw players and coach closer together and provide a better understanding between them. Coaches who spend time developing an empathy with their players will learn to recognize and understand their feelings of anxiety, anger, frustration and enjoyment. This will promote communication which should help to remove many problems which may inhibit performance.

Coaches will also gain insight into the feelings that players have when they perform poorly. If their loss of self-esteem is understood, it is obvious not to compound problems by undermining them when they are already down. Communicating respect to one's players will more likely lead to reciprocal treatment and understanding. Having empathy with them is a key factor in this.

The Role of the Coach

Within a sport a team coach is a 'co-ordinator of playing resources' as well as an 'educator' of players. Some coaches may only be involved with an individual or a few players and therefore orientate themselves primarily to the 'educator' function. All hockey coaches, no matter what their primary function or their level of performance, have an important part to play and role to perform.

While coaches are often expected to have a plethora of attributes, their principal areas of responsibility are the following:

1. Technical. The teaching and practising of techniques relevant to the game.
2. Strategic. The utilization of these techniques in the development of strategies to gain ascendency over the opposition. These manifest themselves at individual, group and team levels in the roles of players and methods of play.

3. Tactical. The use of certain strategies in the game situation against particular opponents or in particular situations.
4. Physiological. The development of the physiological attributes of players with reference to their age, strengths and the demands of the game.
5. Psychological. An understanding of the psychological profile of the individual players is essential to helping them achieve maximum performance (motivation).
6. Sociological. A team game is by its very nature a social activity requiring considerable interaction between players aspiring to a common goal.

These areas of essential knowledge will be expanded later in the book, but the reality of any coaching programme is that there are always constraints which inhibit the achievement of the ideal. These enemies appear in the form of restrictions on the availability of time, knowledge, players, facilities and finance.

It is unlikely that *all* areas will be a problem of similar magnitude and the coach (management team) will have to assess the situation carefully and make realistic goals for the players and team during the planned programme. The critical decision-making must relate to the priority placed on the respective areas of work and this in turn is closely associated with the evaluation of the previous programme. Experience suggests that the greater proportion of time is spent on technical, tactical and physiological aspects of preparation with the other areas receiving extra emphasis at specific times (e.g. close to the competition stage) or when circumstances allow (e.g. finance, time, expertise).

For this kind of decision-making to take place, the following planning procedures need to occur over a period of time in each of the areas of responsibility identified.

1. Identification/investigation of an area of work in need of improvement.
2. Construction of a programme to achieve the improvement.

3. Implementation of the programme.
4. Evaluation of the process and its effectiveness.
5. Reassessment of the requirements for future planning.

This simple, but important, series of activities is relevant to work at each of individual, group and team levels. Again, it is unlikely that a coach has the time and facility to work at the individual level for all players, and decisions regarding areas of priority have to be made. However, until the coach outlines clearly the areas and levels of work, these decisions cannot easily be made. This process may create opportunity for success but the key factors in translating potential into performance are knowledge and communication – and this is the real challenge to any coach.

3
THE CHALLENGE OF COACHING

While there are many challenges facing a coach, the *raison d'être* for a coach can be described quite briefly as follows:

> 'To create an environment for the players with whom the coach works which promotes and maximizes performance improvement.'

It is the coach's responsibility to make certain that he has the relevant sport-specific knowledge and coaching skills. The players bring with them their playing attributes, personal qualities and potential. The progress made by these players over time will depend upon the quality of the interaction between them and the coach, that is the quality of the coaching process.

This coaching process, although based upon the knowledge of the coach, hinges on the quality of the learning environment he establishes and develops. The quality of this learning environment is greatly influenced by the communication process between coach and player, and the methods employed to promote performance improvement. These two areas are inevitably closely inter-related and while they are separated here for the purpose of explanation, in reality this is not the case.

Communication

This section identifies *what* coaches have to communicate about and *how* they do it. While it is not possible to look at the art of communication closely, its importance in the coaching process demands some attention.

Coaches have to be able to communicate on a whole range of topics related to the game to a wide range of players. These topics include:

1. Techniques, strategies, tactics and principles.
2. Creating the appropriate environment.
3. Organizing individuals and groups.

The coach will primarily use verbal communication to give and obtain this information, although demonstrations (e.g. physical, video, etc.) are important non-verbal methods of communicating.

The Fundamentals of Verbal Communication

1. The coach must know what he wants to achieve through the communication.
2. He must be clear about what and how much he is going to say.
3. He must plan the timing and order of his comments.
4. He must give clear, concise and relevant information.
5. He must attempt to phrase the information positively at all times.
6. He must use an enthusiastic tone which will motivate listeners.
7. He must decide whether his comments are aimed at individuals, groups or everyone.
8. He must promote responsibility in players for their work.
9. He must illustrate whenever possible that he values the players' work.
10. He must ask for their views, observations and feelings.
11. He must listen to them.

The purpose of this communication between the coach and the players is to maximize performance improvement, that is the players should learn how to perform to a higher standard. It is important, therefore, to link this verbal communication with the learning process.

The Role of Verbal Communication in the Learning Process

Within sport the three principal methods used in the learning process are verbal communication (telling), demonstration (showing) and experience (doing). All three are important and rarely work in isolation, yet many coaches tend to rely very heavily upon telling the performer what to do.

However, there are many examples of people learning to perform to high standards without being told how to do it. Their key learning methods were through watching others and experience.

Also, while telling is a very fast method of sending out information, there is no guarantee that the receiver will understand it. This can only be checked by performance – and how often a coach is heard saying to players: 'How many times must I tell you. . . !'

While telling is very appropriate at times, it is also capable of causing misunderstanding, confusion and frustration in the performer. These will inhibit the development of performance and understanding and do little to promote responsibility.

Asking and Listening

Telling is not the only way of promoting verbal communication; asking and listening are both powerful methods that are greatly underused by coaches.

Asking is not merely meant to check that the performers know what they have been told. Asking can also more effectively draw out knowledge and experience that is particularly relevant to a situation and that assists understanding.

Asking is the difference between 'Move the defender in this direction by running along this line and passing the ball at that point', and 'If we want to use that space, where should we move the defender?' 'How could this be achieved?' 'When could the pass be made?' 'What is the cue for the pass to be given?'

Where the coach dictates and performs, it is questionable w generates awareness and respc the player and whether the pla stands the important concepts ii ment. On the other hand, the very act of asking questions introduces several new dimensions:

1. It illustrates to the player that his knowledge is valued.
2. It heightens awareness of what needs to be done.
3. It generates responsibility.
4. It puts the player at the centre of the learning process.
5. It allows the speed of learning to be at the performer's pace, not the coach's.

All of these involve the player more in the learning process and promote understanding of and commitment to the task. A secondary, yet equally important, skill that must be allied to the questioning, is the listening to the answer. This provides the coach with the cues for the next question.

While the process of asking and listening may at first appear longer, the benefits are considerable. They include being able to apply this process to similar and new situations, and increasing the ability of players to ask themselves and each other effective questions. These in time accelerate the learning process. It is important therefore that coaches examine the amount of telling they use, and its effectiveness, and perhaps consider using more effective questioning, which is an underused technique in the learning environment. If coaches are able to improve the quality and effectiveness of their verbal communication by using appropriate combinations of asking and telling, then the beneficiaries will be their players, the very group they serve.

The Teaching/Coaching Process

Interacting closely with the quality of the communication between coach and

Striving for Effective Questioning

Questioning demands a commitment from the coach to experiment because one's natural inclination is to tell. Most people grow up in an environment dominated by telling. The following points should assist the coach wishing to introduce more questioning:

1. The coach must have a sound understanding of the area of work.
2. The coach should know where the process is leading, yet have an open mind regarding alternative solutions.
3. Listening to the answer will promote subsequent questions.
4. The less judgemental the coach can be, the more positive the progress.
5. It may be easier to begin in areas such as 'developing strategies' where there are clearly several options available.
6. Choose a safe environment in which to start.
7. The questions follow the interest of the player and this interest is shown in the words they use in the answers/observations. The process is ask–listen–reflect.
8. Ask 'open' rather than 'closed' questions. Open questions demand information whereas closed questions demand 'yes' or 'no' answers.
9. Use 'leading' questions as little as possible.
10. The most effective questions start with 'what', 'when', 'where' and 'how much', rather than 'why'.

Effective questioning is an excellent tool for the coach to have in the communications kit and once it is employed skilfully, it allows many situations that were previously approached through telling to be tackled differently and ultimately more effectively.

---

performer is the process used to promote performance improvement. Coaches look for performers who are able to accept the responsibility for their own performance, and who can recognize changing circumstances and respond accordingly. No coaches in any sport actually go through the competitive arena with the performer. They may be close by and interacting with the performer occasionally (at the end of a period of play which may vary from a few minutes up to three quarters of an hour) but they do not have to cope with the competitive situations. Players therefore need to be coached, so that they are able not only to perform all the necessary skills and strategies but also to accept the responsibility as decision-makers to solve the problems in the dynamic environment of the game.

Coaching is an interaction between coach and performer, the former bringing experience of both the game and coaching methodology, while the latter has unique attributes and game experience. The process, therefore, is a dialogue not a monologue; it must be developed so that the attributes and experience of the performer are recognized, valued and utilized to enhance performance. If this dialogue is to be promoted then the method of effective questioning already described becomes a very effective tool.

One of the greatest challenges to a team coach is that of promoting both individual performance and teamwork to the highest level.

The process of utilizing players' experience and knowledge is a vital part of overcoming this potential dichotomy between individual and team. Involving players in the decision-making process by asking for knowledge and experience illustrates this value to them and builds self-esteem. Once this has taken place the needs of the team must be addressed. Although these may not be in harmony with the desires of some of the individual players, they are more likely to be accepted because the process accepts the importance of the individual. In this way, players more easily realize that the team is more important than the individual.

G	Goal	Identify the area of development and the team's specific goals.
R	Reality	Where are the team now? How are they performing? What do they do at present?
O	Options	How can the team get from the present situation to their goal? This is the stage in which the real coaching takes place. Discussions must be open and honest so that players can utilize the shared knowledge and understand one another's difficulties, etc. A range of options are sought and it is advantageous *not* to judge them too quickly.
W	Will	What are the team going to do? When is it going to be done? Who does what? This is the commitment to put into practice the agreed solution(s). It is essential to finalize this, otherwise the purpose of the discussion will not have been fulfilled.

The following is a simple model to help identify issues within the coaching process and take them forward. The model is encapsulated in the word GROW, which is a mnemonic.

This model can be used on a macro scale (in planning a programme) or a micro scale (in investigating strategies in 2 vs 1). In conjunction with effective questioning, it becomes a powerful method of promoting understanding in players.

The Advantages of a Problem-Solving Approach

1. The coach is able to set other problems which do not have clear-cut answers and therefore take performance beyond the personal experience of the players.
2. It promotes the coach to trust the players to cope with the challenges of practice and performance.
3. It allows the coach to focus attention on future developments to enhance performance still further.
4. The players will become decision-makers while still accountable to their colleagues and the coach.
5. The players are challenged to respond to situations without looking to the coach for the solutions.
6. The players will more easily accept responsibility for their own performance.
7. The players will focus their attention on quality work when they are training alone.

The coaching process is a complex matrix, but the most powerful coaching environments are founded on simple yet fundamental principles. It is always worth the time to explore and revisit this area, as it is part of the foundations of what a coach does.

Planning Progressive Practices and Games

Within the learning environment, quality performance depends on three aspects:

1. Well-structured progressions to aid the learning of skills and strategies.
2. Their integration into game-like situations.
3. Progression to the full game.

The sooner the coach is able to put the skill or strategy into a real game-like situation, the more rapid will be the understanding by the players. Having a sound knowledge of the concepts that underpin progressions for practices and games will allow the coach to cater for a wide range of situations and players. The structure can be used for developing a skill, integrating a skill into a strategy, experimenting with a strategy, working on a group issue/exercise or an exercise with the whole team; in fact, almost any situation.

Progressive practices are the means by

which a coach efficiently achieves his objectives in any skill or tactical practice, whether it be with a group or an individual. The planning of these practices is very little documented, yet it is fundamental to the coaching and learning process.

The aim of practising is to enable players to learn, modify and perfect skills and tactical moves so that they are able to reproduce them in the game situation. This means that the skill or tactic has in the end to be performed under stressful conditions; and it will be the degree of stress applied to a practice that provides the progression. There are three types of degree of stress which can be alternated in any practice: competitive, skill and spatial stress.

These will be looked at in more detail.

Competitive Stress

This ranges between non-competitive and competitive and is altered by increasing or decreasing:

1. The level of opposition inhibiting the successful completion of the activity, for example, cones, passive defender, active defender (including perhaps some conditions on movement), passive defenders and active defenders (no conditions).
2. The time available in which to perform the activity once or several times (competition against the clock).
3. The amount of time given between each repetition, for example, one, two or multiple ball practices.

It is, of course, possible to combine these three ways of changing competitive stress, leading to greater sophistication in the progressive practices for any activity along this single pathway.

Skill Stress

Here skills can vary from simple to more complex or difficult. The degree of stress may be increased by the very nature of the skill being learned or practised. An aerial flick, which is intrinsically more difficult

than a pushed pass, can therefore also be affected by demanding more of the player before, during and/or after the performance of the skill.

For example, the stress degree when practising a skill like controlling the ball on the open stick can be increased progressively as follows:

1. The player is stationary.
2. The player receives a ball from various directions.
3. A ball is lifted to the player.
4. The player moves (in various directions) before receiving the ball.
5. As above, plus the player controls the ball and moves on in the same direction.
6. As above, but the player controls the ball and then changes direction with it.
7. The player controls the ball and then passes to predetermined points. This progression can be done with as little or as much preliminary work as the coach desires, for example, the player receives and passes in a stationary position.
8. As above, plus various types of pass or shot at goal.

Note In the example above, the degree of competitive and spatial stress has been kept as constant as possible, but the coach could quite easily develop these simultaneously.

Spatial Stress

This progression is concerned with the space available in which to perform the skill or tactic and obviously develops from an uncongested to a congested situation. The degree of stress is altered by changing the size and/or the shape of the space. However, it is not always the smallest (or most congested) space that provides the most testing conditions for all skills and tactical practices. Consider the principles of defending, whether as an individual or a group. They are more easily practised in space of a limited size or congested by the number of defenders occupying it, and this has important ramifications on progressive practices aimed at improving defensive techniques. The reverse is generally true for attacking techniques, that is, success is more easily attained if the space is large or uncongested.

Through the thoughtful use of these concepts, the coach is able not only to plan accurately a series of progressions that will enable him to achieve pre-determined objectives, but also to quickly and easily modify the progressions so that they are at the appropriate level for the player or players. However, there are two important factors that the coach ignores at his peril:

1. A good series of progressions has only one or two major objectives, as it is very difficult for learning and practising to be effective if there are too many objectives. This is especially important when coaching young or less expert players.
2. There is a subtle difference between preparing progressions for practice and teaching. In the latter, the end product is the successful performance of the skill or tactic in its entirety, whereas practising is the performance of the complete skill or tactic under conditions of increasing stress so that it can be reproduced in the game situation. It is important to recognize and make allowance for this difference when planning a coaching session. For example, when teaching, it is wise to set the spatial stress at a level that maximizes the chance of success, keep the competitive stress to a minimum and make the progressions along the skill pathway.

The following example illustrates how to utilize the methods of GROW, Effective Questioning and Progressive Practices.

Developing the 2 vs 1 Strategy in Attack

First of all, the area to be worked on is identified and confirmed using the GROW model, as follows.

Goal To improve the success rate of creating and completing 2 vs 1 in attack.

Reality Have the players had the opportunities and failed to convert a significant number? What evidence do they have to this effect? Players' views, coach's observations, video? What parts of the movement were breaking down? Recognition of 2 vs 1? Implementation of strategy? All strategies failing, or just one or two? Passer, receiver, or both having difficulties?

Options To leave the strategy as it is and hope it improves, to omit the strategy from the repertoire, to concentrate on a few strategies and do them well, or to review all strategies.

Will To concentrate on a single strategy on each flank. (N.B. In reality this will depend upon the answers to the above questions and others).

Once a specific strategy requiring improvement has been identified, a series of progressive practices should follow to develop the strategy, like the following.

PRACTICE 1
Objective To practise the chosen 2 vs 1 strategy on wings in a good sized area against defenders.
Procedure Detailed work on movement, cues, timing of pass, etc.; questioning the forwards and defenders to find the best solutions; gradually increasing the challenge to the forwards by demanding execution at greater speed, more active defender, control of passes beforehand, reduction in size of area; and using the GROW model to work through difficulties where appropriate.

PRACTICE 2
Objective To work 2 vs 1 within a 3 vs 2 situation.
Procedure Integrating a modified and improved strategy in a large area on the flank; questioning to emphasize how to make it happen in a 3 vs 2 situation; introducing the support of the leading two coming from a deeper position; increasing stress by reducing the size of the area, giving the attackers a time frame and allowing a third defender to tackle back on the support player; demanding that the attacking group get the

Fig 3 Increased pressure on the attack in a 2 vs 1 situation.

ball into the circle under control; as above, but with a goalkeeper and centre forward to test the effectiveness of the strategy and the centre.

PRACTICE 3 Fig 5
Objective   To complete the 2 vs 1 within a 3 vs 2 situation but with increased pressure on the attack.
Procedure   The inside right has to win the ball from the two opponents in a confined area. On winning the ball, the inside right, right half and right wing combine to beat the two defenders in the designated area. Once inside the 25 the central defender can help the other defenders.

The central defender cannot be involved with the centre forward when the ball has entered the circle. A pass to the centre forward is not allowed until the attack is beyond the 16yd line.
Progressions   One of the midfield players can be allowed to tackle back once the attack is inside the 25, or the central defender can assist the other defenders from the outset but

must start from a marking position of the centre forward.

Practices 1–3 focus on the preparation of the strategy, the timing and reasoning for the passes and movements to set up the opportunity.

PRACTICE 4
Objective   To provide the attacking team with the opportunity to set up the strategies against a full defence.
Procedure   There are six attackers against five defenders and a goalkeeper. The attackers seek to set up 2 vs 1 on the flanks to produce an incisive move into the 25 and circle, while the defence win if they clear the ball outside the 25.
Progressions   The attackers must create a shot or penalty corner after the incision, or the defenders win by taking the ball over the quarter or half-way line under control. The progression after this practice is to measure the success rate in the next game situation.

THE WORKSHOP
PART 2

4

CORE SKILLS

The Grips

The position and movement of the hands on the stick are crucial skills in hockey as they can have a significant influence upon a player's performance. While it may be advantageous not to emphasize this aspect of skill development too heavily with beginners, the sooner young players can accommodate the various hand positions and movements, the more rapidly they will progress.

In all striking games which use an implement, the coach faces the dilemma of balancing the introduction of essential fundamentals with the provision of games and enjoyment. In hockey this difficulty can be overcome through clever use of progressive small games or challenges. *See* Chapter 13 (Developing Young Players) for some examples.

Forehand Grip Fig 4

This is the basic grip for running with the ball on the forehand side, controlling the ball on the forehand side and pushing/flicking the ball. The position of the right hand will probably vary between players. The lower the right hand the greater the strength and control *but* the more the player must stoop. As players develop strength, dexterity and confidence in their ball control, so the position of the right hand will change, moving higher up the stick.

Reverse Stick Grip Fig 5

This grip is used for moving the ball from left to right, and controlling the ball on the reverse stick side. Notice how the right hand position has not altered, the stick being allowed to turn through the hand. The left hand has turned the stick.

Striking the Ball Fig 6

Bringing the hands together allows the stick to be moved quickly in both backswing and downswing to propel the ball with greater speed.

Fig 4 Forehand grip.

(a)　　　　　　　　　　　　　(b)

Fig 5 Reverse stick grip.

(a)

(b)

Fig 6 Striking the ball.

(a)

(b)

While these are the basic hand positions there are subtle variations according to the skills being performed. This is particularly so with the left hand and coaches must be aware of these alterations.

Moving the Ball

Within the game there are many patterns of movement of the player with the ball in his own space. These movements are used to create space so that a passing, shooting or dribbling opportunity can be realized. There are endless variations on these simple patterns and practising is essential to develop harmony of movement and therefore efficiency.

PATTERN 1 Fig 7
The ball is transferred from left to right and dribbled forward on the forehand. Body weight starts on the left side and transfers with the ball. Once the ball is on the forehand stick the player can scan for passes.
Common faults The body moves before the ball, making the movement more difficult.

PATTERN 2 Fig 8
The same pattern as pattern 1 but the ball is lifted forward to beat a low reverse stick tackle. The key part of the skill pattern is the point at which the ball is played forward. The ball is ahead of the right foot and the player drops the right hand side of the body slightly to allow the stick to get beneath the ball.

The lifting of the ball is dominated by the right hand. As the ball is lifted into the air the body weight is transferred forward.
Common faults The body weight is transferred forward too soon; the ball is too wide of the right foot to lift forward; or the body is too upright to lift the ball.

Fig 7 Moving the Ball 1.

(a)

(b)

(c)

(d)

Fig 8 Moving the Ball 2.

(a)

(b)

(c)

(d)

Fig 9 Moving the Ball 3.

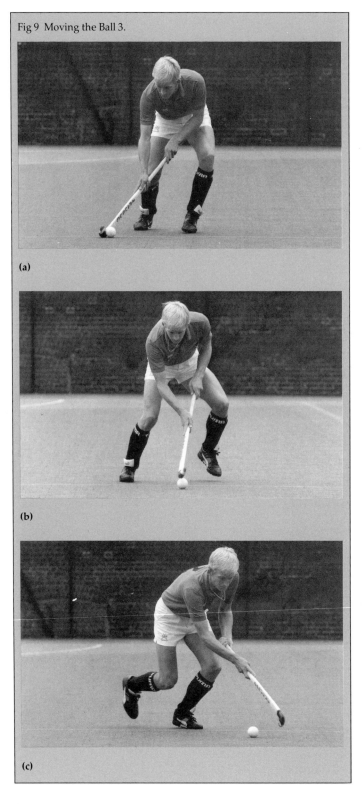

(a)

(b)

(c)

PATTERN 3 Fig 9

The ball is moved from right to left with the forehand, controlled outside the left foot with the reverse stick and then dribbled forward.

The body weight transfers from right to left and then forwards.

Common faults The ball is not allowed to travel far enough to the player's left, or the ball is not controlled by the reverse stick with the body weight on the left foot.

PATTERN 4 Fig 10

The ball is switched from right to left and then lifted forward with the reverse stick. The ball may have to be controlled before it is lifted forward, although it is advantageous to allow the ball to roll onto the reverse stick. The stick needs to be angled so that the ball can be lifted.

Common faults The player attempts to perform the skill too quickly, or the stick is too upright, making it difficult to lift the ball.

PATTERN 5 Fig 11

The ball is transferred from right to left and then diagonally backwards before being dribbled forwards on the forehand stick. The crucial part of the movement is when the ball is dragged diagonally back. The position of the left foot is outside the ball, allowing space for the ball to move backwards and the body to pivot on the left foot.

The skill is constantly used by players when they are being pressured by an opponent and forced to move to their left with the ball.

The angle at which the ball is moved from left to right can vary according to the situation.

The player can even pretend to pull the ball backwards and dribble forwards into space.

Common faults Incorrect

Fig 10 Moving the Ball 4.

(a)

(b)

(c)

Fig 11 Moving the Ball 5.

(a)

(b)

(c)

Fig 12 Moving the ball 6.

(a)

(b)

(c)

(d)

(e)

(f)

foot positioning; moving the body too quickly; leaving the ball behind in the movement; or not keeping the stick close to the ball to facilitate the smoothness of the pattern.

PATTERN 6 Fig 12

The ball is moved back with the reverse stick and then dragged from right to left with the forehand stick.

Control to the left is done with the reverse stick and then the ball is dribbled forward. The pivot is done with the weight on the right foot; while this foot does not have to be outside the line of the ball, it must be beyond the point at which the ball is controlled to alter its direction – this is in order that there is space for the ball to be moved from right to left.

Common faults Incorrect foot positions in relation to the ball.

PATTERN 7

The ball is taken diagonally back from right to left with the forehand stick and then dragged from left to right with the reverse stick before being dribbled forward. The pivot is done on the left foot as in pattern 5 and the angle of the movement can vary according to the demands of the situation.

This pattern of movement can be utilized by players in both attacking and defending positions.

All these patterns and those that many coaches can develop for themselves can be built upon by introducing body and stick feints within the movement.

The key to finding the appropriate movement for any particular situation is to introduce an opponent who seeks to pressurize the person with the ball. It is the responsibility of the player in

Fig 13   Stephen Batchelor shows quality control during the Seoul Olympics.

possession to recognize the position and movement of the opponent and set up an appropriate variation of these patterns to provide them with the opportunity for success. The best coaches will be able to guide the players so that they can get the maximum out of this type of practice, for it is too easy for the player without the ball to destroy the exercise.

The defender can be directed initially to approach the player with the ball in specific directions to enable the attacker to choose the most appropriate pattern of movement.

Controlling the Ball

Good control of the ball when it is being passed from colleague to colleague or intercepted is of paramount importance as it provides a team with the opportunity to maintain or instigate attacking moves. Poor control tips the scales in favour of the opposition and will result in colleagues lacking the confidence to make movements off the ball to lead or support players.

The Basic Principles of Controlling the Ball

While there are many minor variations of body, stick and foot positions according to the situation, the vast majority of instances concerning controlling the ball can be assisted by the adherence to a number of common-sense principles:

1. Watch the ball on to the stick. Focusing attention on other matters such as the position and movement of colleagues and opponents should be done before and after control. The more experienced and confident the player the more relevant information he will be able to assimilate while focusing on the ball.
2. Eyes and stick in line with the ball. It is advantageous to achieve this as early as possible in the process of controlling the ball. In reality it can often occur only quite late in the movement as the ball may be passed while the player is moving into the path of the ball.
3. At the point of control the stick is comparatively stationary. Moving the stick across the line of the ball or jabbing it toward the ball will make the control considerably more difficult.
4. The stick 'gives' to cushion the ball. This 'feel' for the ball is probably experienced more in the right hand than the left but there is no doubt that both hands are involved. Holding the stick just above the surface of the field facilitates this part of the skill.
5. A more upright stance allows rapid change of direction. On surfaces other than artificial turf a more vertical stick can help control as it provides for the more uneven run of the ball. On artificial turf the smoothness of the surface allows players to control the ball with a more horizontal stick position. While this has advantages there are also potential difficulties.
6. The receiver should be in a balanced position at the point of collection. This does not mean a stationary position because this is not always possible or appropriate. Balanced means that the body is under control so that attention can be focused on the positioning of feet, hands, head, trunk and stick to give maximum opportunity for successful control and subsequent movement. Balance will also allow the receiver to use stick and body feints to deceive the opponent.
7. Positioning the ball for the next movement. The culmination of the application of these basic principles is that the receiver creates the opportunity to dribble, shoot or pass, so maintaining the attacking movement. The earlier in their careers that players can plan ahead by practising the positioning of the ball for the next movement, then the more effective they will be in the match situation.

RECEIVING THE BALL FROM AHEAD Figs 14–16
All the basic principles identified previously are being applied to this situation (Fig 14): position of hands, stick, body and eyes. The final picture shows the movement of feet in preparation for the next skill the player wishes to perform, emphasizing that in most situations the ball is repositioned rather than stopped dead.

On the forehand stick In the situation in Fig 15 the ball has had to be controlled with an upright stick close to or outside the left foot. This skill is often needed when an opponent is attempting to exploit the relative weakness of this area. The body weight transfers to the left foot to enable the player to get the stick and his eyes as close to the line of the ball as possible. As soon as control is gained he moves the ball to the right into a stronger position.

The secondary movement could be directly forward or to the player's left, according to the situation, and players must practise all these alternatives. It is also important to vary the kind of pass the player has to control in this position so that he can cope with a wide variety of situations.

On the reverse stick When the reverse stick control is appropriate the player pivots on the right foot so that the right shoulder turns toward the ball (Fig 16). This allows the stick and eyes to get close to the line of the ball. The ball is controlled near the line of the left foot depending to a large extent on the planned subsequent move of the player (refer to the movement patterns described earlier).

Common faults These are almost inevitably associated with the basic principles described at the beginning of

Fig 14 Receiving the ball from ahead.

(a)

(b)

(c)

Fig 15 Receiving the ball ahead on the forehand stick.

(a)

(b)

(c)

Fig 16 Receiving the ball from ahead on the reverse stick.

(a)

(b)

(c)

this section. It is always advisable to look at each of these principles carefully before examining more complex reasons why control may be less than satisfactory.

RECEIVING THE BALL FROM THE LEFT Figs 17, 19 and 21
On the forehand stick   There are two methods of receiving. In the first (Fig 17), the player's chest faces the ball and the ideal point of control is between the feet or by the right foot. This technique allows the player to get his eyes, stick and body behind the line of the ball, giving himself maximum opportunity to control the pass, but because this position cannot be taken up while moving forwards emphasis must be put upon quickly repositioning the ball and body immediately after the ball has been controlled. This skill is often used by players when they have come back quickly toward their own goal to escape from a tight marking opponent.

The second method (Fig 19) is only slightly different but it allows the receiver to be moving forward as he controls the ball. As the player is running forward, the chest cannot be turned much toward the ball but the eyes and stick get in line with the pass through the natural forward lean of the body. The ball is controlled to the right of the line of the left foot and it is important to get the foot pattern in harmony with the control, so that the player is able to perform a subsequent predetermined movement. The game situation is rarely such that a player can receive the ball in a stationary position unhindered by the opposition. In reality, players have to develop more advanced skills based upon the basic concepts outlined above. They may have to control the ball at full stretch

Fig 17 Receiving the ball from the left on the forehand stick 1.

(a)   (b)

Fig 18   Miskimmin of New Zealand cuts through the Pakistan midfield during their clash in
the 1986 World Cup. New Zealand led 3–1 only to lose 4–3 in the final few minutes.

Fig 19 Receiving the ball from the left on the forehand stick 2.

(a)

(b)

(c)

or at full running speed. The situation may demand that they move toward the ball or let it run across their body before controlling it.

The choice of which method to use will depend upon a variety of factors including the type of pitch, the speed and quality of the pass, the position of the opposition and the position and movement of colleagues.

On the reverse stick   All players must be able to control passes on the reverse side, even when they come from the left, as not every pass will be totally accurate or it may be the only line of pass available to the passer. (For technique, see Receiving the Ball from the Right). The important point for players receiving these passes is that they must turn quickly to face the opposition so that they do not obstruct. Advanced players have found that it is possible to use a pass from left to right aimed deliberately at the reverse stick without producing obstruction. As the attacker moves away from the defender the ball is passed to the reverse side and the receiver turns anticlockwise as he controls it and then dribbles upfield (Fig 21). Note the point at which the attacking player receives the ball. This is a highly skilful move and requires excellent timing to avoid obstruction. Inside rights use it frequently against tight-marking opponents.

The recent modifications to the interpretation of the obstruction rules have given the player in possession greater freedom in the skill of controlling a pass and turning to face the opposition.

Fig 20   The West German forward shows high-quality control at speed against Spain in the 1988 Seoul Olympics.

Fig 21   Receiving the ball from the left on the reverse stick.

RECEIVING THE BALL FROM THE RIGHT Figs 22–25

On the reverse stick   This skill is used when the receiver has space ahead of him in which to move, for receiving on the reverse stick demands constant attention on the ball. This makes it longer before the player can scan ahead for further passes. The body weight is forward with the right shoulder toward the ball, and at the point of contact the left foot is usually forward, allowing the eyes to be as close as possible to the line of the pass. The ball is controlled in front of or even outside the line of the left foot to allow the forward movement to be maintained. As players become more confident, they should be able to control passes further ahead using the left hand only (Fig 23).

43

Fig 22 Receiving the ball from the right on the reverse stick.

(a)

(b)

(c)

Fig 23 Receiving the ball from the right on the reverse stick, using one hand.

(a)

(b)

Fig 24 Receiving the ball from the right on the forehand stick while stationary or moving away from the goal.

Common faults The player attempts to control the ball too close to the feet or nearer the line of the right foot, which will inhibit the flow of the move and even deflect the ball back into the feet.

On the forehand stick This skill is often used when the player is stationary or moving away from the goal (Fig 24), usually in a congested area (for example, the circle) or when a player is being marked tightly. The player moves away from the defender and receives the pass from the right onto his forehand stick. At the moment of control the player must ideally be well balanced with knees slightly bent, feet apart with the chest facing the ball, although generally the body weight tends to be over the right leg (Fig 24). The ball is controlled in front of or outside the right foot.

It is very important that the receiver develops nimble footwork, body movement and skilful ball positioning to minimize the chances of the defender being able to tackle him.

Where the receiver moves forward, he twists the upper part of his body toward the ball, and collects the pass on the forehand stick quite close to his feet (Fig 25).

These forehand techniques are particularly useful when players are closely marked, when the area is congested, or when possession with the ball in a strong position to pass or dribble is a high priority.

The advantage of this movement is that the player can lift his eyes sooner to scan for passes and he is in a strong position to pass, dribble or shoot. The loss of vision to the player's left is, of course, a difficulty but this skill is utilized because of a lack of space ahead of the player, the desire to return a pass to the right or the

Fig 25 Receiving the ball from the right on the forehand stick while moving forward.

(a)

(b)

(c)

Fig 26 Receiving from behind on the forehand stick.

(a)

(b)

(c)

pass ahead to the reverse stick was not possible. If the receiver has time he can quickly position the ball ahead and scan to his left for passes. In Fig 25(a) the stick is quite angled, but this can vary considerably without loss of effectiveness.

RECEIVING FROM BEHIND
Figs 26 and 27

On the forehand stick This skill is often used to evade a tight-marking defender and utilize the space between the attacker and the passer of the ball to retain possession (Fig 26). The initial part of the movement may be very fast but good balance is essential at the point of control for the ball has to be taken back toward its origin. The arms and hands have to have excellent feel for the ball to be able to control it. The point of control is ahead of the body and/or outside the line of the right foot.

On the reverse stick This skill can be completed while moving away from a defender and toward the origin of the ball but there are distinct advantages if the receiver can be moving forward (upfield) as he controls the ball. The pass can be taken in stride, particularly if the defender is infield of the receiver and therefore on his reverse stick. A further advantage is the distance the pass can be taken away from the body and therefore the defender. Some players look to receive this pass with a very horizontal stick. While this can be useful if the pass is wayward, the low position of the receiver makes subsequent movements more difficult.

Players manipulate the best receiving position by taking defenders away from the area that they wish to utilize and moving in a curve when they make the leading run (Fig 27).

Fig 27 Receiving from behind on the reverse stick

(a) (b)

Fig 28   Manipulating the best receiving position.

Common faults The pass is not taken level with or ahead of the left foot, causing it to deflect toward the feet of the receiver, or the pass is controlled too close to the feet, inhibiting the movement of the receiver.

CONTROLLING THE AERIAL BALL Figs 29–32

Aerial passes are most commonly used in two ways: as an incisive pass into space behind defenders or to a specific defender in order to pressure that player into an error.

In either case it is important that the defender nearest the ball has the skill and confidence to control the ball as it descends.

On the forehand stick The player is in a stationary position (Fig 29 (a)). The hands are apart on the stick and the body is in a well-balanced position in preparation not only for the control of the ball but also any necessary subsequent movement. The concentration is on the ball and the eyes and stick are in line with the path of the ball.

The point of control is preferably around waist height with the head of the stick farther from the body than the handle (Fig 29 (b)). Control is made on the blade below the right hand and it is this hand that cushions the impact. The position of the hand and arm allow the stick to give as the ball makes contact.

The ball has dropped gently to the ground at a comfortable position in front of the feet, and the player moves into space away from any possible pressure from opponents, hoping to steal the ball once it is grounded (Fig 29 (c)).

On the reverse stick This is done while the player moves toward the line of the ball so that he can get his stick and eyes as near as possible along this line (Fig 30 (a)). The stick is positioned in the path of the ball as early as possible with the hands apart to cushion the impact. While the player has to move to get the ball he maintains good balance through using relatively short steps.

The ball is collected and dropped to the side of the body ready for the next move (Fig 30 (b)). If the player were attacking he could continue his run forward. If he were defending, on the other hand,

Fig 29 Controlling the aerial ball on the forehand stick.

(a) (b) (c)

Fig 30   Controlling the aerial ball on the reverse stick.

(a)

(b)

Fig 31 Controlling the aerial ball 1.

(a) (b)

Fig 32 Controlling the aerial ball 2.

(a) (b)

(c)

he could quickly pivot and put the ball onto his stronger side.

Once the basic technique has been mastered the receiver can develop this skill to an even higher level by taking the ball into space with the first touch.

Two examples are shown in Figs 31 and 32. These photographs should be studied carefully before considering the following questions: What modifications are required in the technique to achieve the objective? When would the skill be used? In what other directions would a player like to be able to take the ball using these skills?

Moving with the Ball

FOREHAND DRIBBLE Figs 33–35
The ball is carried ahead of and to the right of the feet. The

(c)

Fig 33   Forehand dribble

(a)

(b)

(c)

body is stooped by slightly lowering the hips as well as bending forward, so that the eyes are in a position to scan for passes, etc. The hands are apart but the position of the right hand will vary according to personal preference. A higher right hand position will raise the body position and assist vision but it may reduce the 'feel' for the ball.

The actual position of the ball may vary according to the situation. When running through space the ball may be ahead and even in a loose dribble, the ball being tapped ahead rather then kept close to the stick. In more congested situations the ball will be carried further back, probably level with the feet.

Players should practise accelerating and decelerating, keeping the ball in the most advantageous position according to the situation.

Right to left and straighten
There are times in the game when a player wishes to move from right to left with the ball on the forehand stick and then go forward again without using the reverse stick.

While the change of direction from sideways to forward may not be as quick when only the forehand stick is used, the ball is always in a strong position, the player's eyes can scan for passes, and rapid acceleration can be included in the movement as the body moves behind the ball.

The movement is achieved through good balance and high-quality footwork. The point of change from a sideways to a forward movement is initiated by turning the upper part of the body to the right as in Fig 34 (c) and (d). This allows the legs to be positioned for forward acceleration if required.

Many young players begin this movement too fast with the result that they struggle to move the body behind the ball without checking the movement of the ball and are unable to accelerate effectively in the latter part of the pattern.

This skill is one that not only develops good balance and footwork but also promotes scanning for passes with the ball close to the stick. In the game it can be used to move defenders sideways and backward with the attacker being able to watch the opponent all the while.

(d)

(e)

Fig 34   Forehand dribble: right to left and straighten.

(a)

(b)

(c)

(d)

54

Fig 35 Forehand dribble, check and move on.

(a)

(b)

(c)

(d)

Check and move on   The ball is carried ahead of the body and outside the line of the right foot. Without decelerating the player checks the forward movement of the ball. As this is achieved the player's feet are closer to but still behind the ball. The player can look up to assess any changes in the game situation and is in a position to pass or change direction without much variation in his running speed. The check can be performed with either left or right foot on the ground without any major disadvantage to the subsequent movement.

This skill can be used to catch a defender off balance as he tries to close down or jab tackle the attacker. Players learning this skill all too often carry the ball too close to the line of their feet with the result that when they check the forward movement of the ball they overrun it. Encourage the body to be stooped with the trunk and stick angled so that the ball is ahead of the body.

Common fault   The ball is

carried in an inappropriate position, so reducing vision or control. An understanding by the coach of the effects of ball position on running speed is essential if players are to maximize both control of the ball while running and their speed.

INDIAN DRIBBLE Fig 36
This skill enables a player to move the ball quickly from left to right and is the basis of all deception when running with the ball. It is of greatest use when beating a player or working in a congested area, especially when accompanied by body and stick feints.

The ball is moved across the front of the body by alternately playing the ball with the forehand and reverse stick. The left hand constantly rotates the stick over the ball,

Fig 36   Indian dribble

(a)

(b)

Basic Dribbling Points
Good coaches will spend time with less experienced players making certain their technique is sound. Some of the most common faults are:

1.   An incorrect grip with the left hand. The V between thumb and index finger should be facing more to the right than the front and the player ought to be able to see the back of the hand and three knuckles.
2.   The ball is too close to the feet restricting bodily movement and scanning.
3.   Scanning (visual awareness of what is ahead and to the side) is sacrificed to continual focus on the ball. Scanning should be positively encouraged during the skill-learning stage.
4.   The ball is only carried directly in front of the feet.
5.   The ball is out of control too often.
6.   The arms do not move with the stick as it moves across the body.

As players develop greater confidence in their dribbling, so they can be led by the coach into more challenging areas that will provide them with a wider range of options to use in the game situation. These will probably include:

1.   Scanning for passes when dribbling.
2.   Changing direction while dribbling without losing balance and the flow of the movement.
3.   Switching the ball quickly from one side of the body to the other.
4.   Body and stick feints within the movements.
5.   Accelerating and decelerating without losing control.

These developments must be introduced in a logical sequence so that learning is facilitated (see Progressive Practices on page 25).

while the right hand allows the stick to turn and combines with the left during the tapping action that changes the direction of the ball. When the ball is moved across the front of the body the arms also move, taking the stick across with the ball.

In Fig 36 (a)–(c) a player performs this dribble with the ball on the left side of the body, and in Fig 36 (d)–(f) on the right side of the body. The ball can also be moved from side to side in front of the feet and the more accomplished players can increase the range of the movement so that they can move the ball at will from either extreme flank to the other.

Common fault   During the Indian dribble it is very difficult to scan for passes when the ball is played with the reverse stick, as the eyes must focus primarily on stick and ball. It is therefore

(c)

(d)

inappropriate to use this kind of dribble when running through space as the player's focus has to return to the ball too often when it could be more usefully employed.

Dragging the Ball

While this is without doubt a core skill the various methods are primarily used for beating an opponent. There are therefore two aspects to the overall skill: the technique of dragging the ball and the strategic aspect of creating and/or recognizing the opportunity to use the skill to beat an opponent. Both areas will be considered within this section but it is important for coaches to recognize that it is easier for players to learn them separately. There are also considerable advantages to developing the teaching of beating an opponent (1 vs 1) from the 2 vs 1 situation. The principal reason for this is that

(e)

(f)

Fig 37   Right to left drag 1.

(a)

(b)

(c)

(d)

(e)

(f)

many of the best opportunities to beat an opponent individually are borne out of a situation in which the defender is not in the ideal position; a reality that the 2 vs 1 situation often creates in a small area with the minimal use of personnel. The simplicity of this situation also promotes recognition and understanding in players which is crucial in the development of their decision-making ability.

RIGHT TO LEFT DRAG Figs 37 and 39

Situation 1   The ball is carried to the right of the body but in the preparation to move rapidly to the left it is usually ahead of the right foot (Fig 37 (a)). Strategically, the aim is to draw the defender to the left, seeking a tackle or the interception of a pass.

As the ball is dragged the body weight is on the right foot, but with a clear body lean to the left (Fig 37 (b)). This allows the body to follow the ball as quickly as possible. The optimum distance from the defender for this movement will depend upon the movement of the players and the situation. Experience will promote this decision-making.

Strategically, the defender should be committed both visually and physically to his left, thus opening up space on the other flank. Moving the ball successfully across the forehand stick of the defender demands that it is done quickly (Fig 37 (c)). In order to regain control the stick stays as close to the ball as possible, in this case with only the left hand in contact, and the left leg steps as far as possible in the first step after the change of direction.

As the ball is collected the body weight and drive of the right leg should allow forward movement to continue immediately (Fig 37 (d)). The ball has been moved about 1½–2 m quickly across the defender and it is now being played beyond the line of the defender's feet, making a recovery much more difficult.

Once the ball is back under control, both hands return to the stick. The ball is manœuvred to a position in which the attacker can continue the forward movement, while scanning to reassess the situation (Fig 37 (e)–(f)). It is at this point that the player can choose to accelerate or decelerate the movement according to the situation. Another advantageous move is to cut to the right to block any recovery movement of the defender.

Fig 38   Karsten Fischer attempts to combat the one-handed open dribble of a Polish forward in the 1986 World Cup, London.

Situation 2 This situation is slightly different in that the attacker is not running directly at the defender. The latter is positioned infield of the attacker, possibly threatening a pass to another player. The defender is probably less worried about the forehand side, as he considers himself capable of covering the attacker's run in that direction. The forward movement is not rapid in this particular situation; strategically, it is therefore the change of direction that is going to be the key to success (Fig 39 (a)). Because the incisive movement will be across the forehand stick and the defender is well balanced, the preparation phase is crucial. The emphasis is on looking for the pass to the defender's left. The ball is carried level with or behind the line of the right foot, while the line of movement of the attacker is toward the defender's right side.

As the defender's stick and weight move to the left the attacker drags the ball from right to left, but because the movement of the ball is more forward than across the field he is quickly beyond the defender (Fig 39 (b)).

The movement with the reverse stick is to get the ball quickly into a position so that he can scan for the next situation.

LEFT TO RIGHT DRAG Fig 40
The ball is carried just outside the right foot, with eyes scanning to take in movement of the defender (Fig 40 (a)). The line of attack is toward the defender's right shoulder. It can be outside this but then more complex alternatives come into play.

The aim is to shift the defender's weight to the right or even force him to move a

Fig 39   Right to left drag 2.

(a)

(b)

(c)

(d)

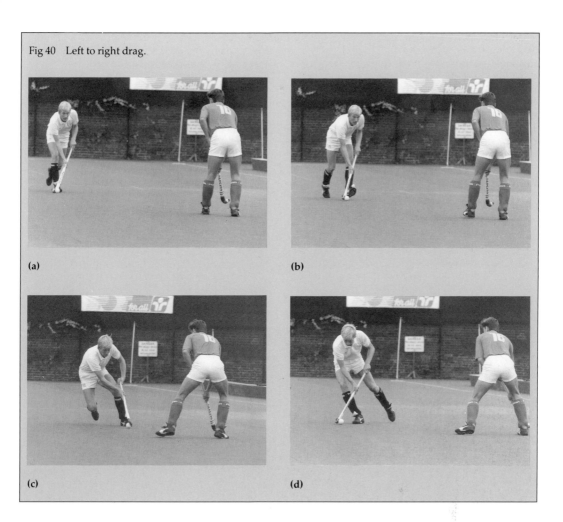

Fig 40 Left to right drag.

(a)

(b)

(c)

(d)

little in that direction. The focus of the attacker is still on ball and defender. The ball is moved in front of the feet, making as if to go to the defender's right (Fig 40 (b)).

As the defender shifts, the ball is dragged from left to right using the reverse stick (Fig 40 (c)). The body weight is on the left foot which drives the body to the right to follow the ball.

The right leg follows the ball to allow the stick to stay close to the ball and continue the forward movement as quickly as possible (Fig 40 (d)). As the attacker goes beyond the line of the feet of the defender, it can be advantageous to cut to

the left so blocking any recovery move that the defender attempts to make.

LEFT TO RIGHT DOUBLE DRAG Fig 41

The attacker drags the ball from left to right but the defender has recovered from the initial deception and prepares to block the move (Fig 41 (a)).

The attacker's forward path is not clear but he has retained composure and balance so that he can respond to the defender's movement (Fig 41 (b)). At this point there is often a slight forward movement with the ball to promote the defender's commitment and

allow good foot positioning.

As the defender commits to the horizontal blocking tackle the attacker drags the ball a second time from left to right (Fig 41 (c)). Here the left leg crosses over the right. This is not incorrect but does not allow as large a step sideways. The defender is forced to stretch even further, allowing the attacker to go around the stick and forward to beat him (Figs 41 (d) and (e)).

Alternatively, in Fig 41 (d) the attacker could lift the ball over the defender's stick into the space beyond or even play the ball back through the feet area where there is little to stop a pass.

Fig 41   Left to right double drag.

(a)

(b)

(c)

(d)

(e)

Passing the Ball

Pushing

This is the most common pass in modern hockey, particularly with the ever-increasing use of artificial turf. Players should be able to use this skill to pass the ball in any direction without giving the opposition notice of their intention. While the stroke lacks the power of the hit, the degree of deception that can be attached to it and the short time between conception and execution more than make up for this in most situations. The reverse stick push is illustrated in the 2 vs 1 situation on page 126.

PUSHING WHILE IN A STATIONARY POSITION Fig 42 The ball is to the right of the body (Fig 42 (a)). The hands are apart on the stick and the body weight transfers from the right to the left foot during the stroke. The eyes are on the ball and the body is in a low powerful position.

The power in the stroke comes from a combination of the transfer of the body weight and the action of the arms (Fig 42 (b)). As the right arm pushes forward the left hand pulls the top of the handle backward causing the head of the stick to accelerate.

The right arm keeps on the line of the ball for as long as possible, so controlling the direction of the pass (Fig 42 (c)). The body stays low to make sure that the power generated by the body action is utilized in the pass.

While it is rarely possible to perform the ideal body movements in the game situation, the understanding of the key principles that influence any skill will enable players to approach optimum performance under the stresses of competition.

Fig 42   Pushing while in a stationary position.

(a)

(b)

(c)

Fig 43   Pushing from right to left while moving forward.

(a)

(b)

(c)

PUSHING WHILE MOVING FORWARD Figs 43 and 44

Right to left   The ball is carried ahead of and to the right of the feet so that the player can maintain good vision (Fig 43 (a)). The body is stooped with the hands apart on the stick (*see* Moving with the Ball on page 51).

The pass, in this case forward and to the left, is made as the right foot comes down onto the ground (Fig 43 (b)). In order to get power behind the ball the right foot is planted almost level with the ball. The right arm is slightly bent.

The ball is passed as the body weight is moving over the right foot, making use of the forward momentum (Fig 43 (c)). The right arm extends in a short powerful movement and the right wrist also extends. At the same time the left hand pulls back to accelerate the head of the stick.

When passing square or even backward to the left, the position of the ball in relation to the right foot will alter so that it will be ahead of or even slightly to the left of that foot. These passes are rarely as powerful as the previous ones as the direction of the pass is different from that of the body and most of the power has to come from the arms alone.

Left to right   The ball is carried on the right of the body with the hands apart in the pushing/dribbling position (Fig 44 (a)). The head begins the left to right rotation of the body.

The upper part of the body turns into position while the right leg turns outward to provide an excellent foundation for the pass (Fig 44 (b)). The arms and hands have moved the stick behind the ball so that the momentum of the ball and body movement is not lost (Fig 44 (c)). The right foot is now the platform for the execution of the pass.

Fig 44 Pushing from left to right while moving forward.

(a)

(b)

(c)

(d)

(e)

(f)

The body has now turned 90 degrees. The left foot steps toward the ball's target and the arms begin to propel the ball (Fig 44 (d)) although the left shoulder may not get all the way round to face the target.

The left foot is now grounded (Fig 44 (e)). The right arm pushes the head of the stick forward while the left begins to pull back the handle to accelerate the head.

The ball has gone but the stick stays on the line of the pass and the body remains low to make sure that the power has been used to propel the ball (Fig 44 (f)).

Fig 45 Left to right pass with the right foot leading.

(a)

(b)

Fig 46 Left to right pass with the reverse stick.

(a)

(b)

(c)

(c)

LEFT TO RIGHT PASS Figs 45 and 46

Right foot leading The technique should be evaluated using the evidence in Fig 45. Here are some questions that may help:

How is the body turn achieved?
Where is the right foot positioned in relation to the ball?
How is the power put into the pass?

Reverse stick Prior to the pass being made the ball is moved to a position in front of the feet (Fig 46 (a)). There is not a very large margin for error in the positioning of the ball with respect to the intended direction of the pass.

The stick is turned to the reverse side and taken away in a short backswing before tapping the ball in the desired direction (Fig 46 (b)).

As the left foot lands, the stick plays through the ball toward the target with the tapping action (Fig 46 (c)). There is no whipping action through the use of the wrist action as in the forehand push. The power is determined by the speed that the player can generate with the arms during the short downswing.

The Flick Figs 47 and 48

This skill, used to project the ball in the air, is popular both in open play and in shooting at goal.

Left foot leading The body weight starts on the right foot. (Fig 47 (a)). The hands are apart but the stronger the player's wrists the closer the right hand can be to the top of the handle. The stick is angled backward so that the head can be positioned behind and beneath the ball.

The left foot steps forward

67

Fig 47 The flick with left foot leading.

(a)

and is placed alongside or just backward of the ball (Fig 47 (b)). The body lowers so that the path of the stick and the power is through the ball and upward. On artificial turf it is possible to step beyond the ball and drag the ball a little before the flick is executed. This can produce extra pace for shooting at goal.

The ball is carried on the

Fig 48 The flick with right foot leading.

(a)   (b)

(c)

stick and the pulling back of the left hand accelerates the stick head just prior to the ball leaving the stick, providing extra power to the flick (Fig 47 (c)). The path of the stick will determine the trajectory of the ball.

(c)

Right foot leading The stick is angled backward with the hands apart (Fig 48 (a)). The body is low to get beneath the ball and the right leg begins to step forward. The right foot provides the platform from which the ball is lifted by the stick (Fig 48 (b)). The ball is kept on the stick for as long as possible. At the very last moment the left wrist pulls the handle backward to accelerate the head to add extra power (Fig 48 (c)).

The Scoop Fig 49
This skill is used to lift the ball high over relatively short distances. The right foot and right shoulder are forward and the hands are apart (Fig 49 (a)).

The right foot is placed alongside and just behind the line of the ball. The right hand position is such that the stick can be lifted through the ball.

Fig 49   The scoop.

(a)   (b)

The left leg drives the body weight forward and the stick lifts the ball (Fig 49 (b)). The eyes stay on the ball and the arms swing forward and upward to give the ball the high trajectory.

The Hit Figs 50 and 51

The hit is used when the speed of the ball is more important than deception. Examples include a long pass to penetrate a defence or switch the direction of play and shooting at goal both in open play and at penalty corners.

In all but shooting at goal it is vital that players can strike the ball smoothly across the surface at the appropriate pace.

Left foot leading   The hands are together near the top of the stick with the left shoulder facing the target (Fig 50 (a)). The body weight begins on the left foot and the left foot steps toward the ball. The stick has been taken back with the arms and the wrists cocked.

The left foot is placed alongside the ball with the leg slightly bent (Fig 50 (b)). The left shoulder still faces the target and the body weight has shifted to the left leg (Fig 50 (c)). The arms are beginning their downward path but the head of the stick is still quite high due to the cocking of the wrists.

The upper part of the body is turning as the arms pull the stick down toward the ball (Fig 50 (d)). The wrists now extend to accelerate the head of the stick so that maximum speed is achieved at impact. The head remains still with the eyes on the ball.

The shoulders have turned further so that the right arm can come through powerfully (Fig 50 (c) and (d)). The stick stays on the line of the ball for as long as possible and the head remains still.

Really powerful strikers have high-quality timing in their hitting techniques, utilizing body and muscular movements to maximize efficiency. While it is important to be able to strike the ball powerfully when required, it is imperative that players can recognize the length of backswing necessary for each situation so that they are effective. Players should also practise both the accuracy of their hitting and deception in the pass. Both of these are achieved through developing high-quality footwork that will maintain good balance and control of the arm and wrist movements which influence direction.

Fig 50   The hit with left foot leading.

(a)

(b)

(c)

(d)

Fig 51 The hit with right foot leading.

(a)

(b)

(c)

(d)

(e)

(f)

72

Right foot leading As the right foot is placed alongside or even slightly ahead of the ball, the upper body is turned so that the left shoulder is pointing toward the target (Fig 51 (a) and (d)). The arms have taken the stick back and the wrists are cocked.

At impact the arms have accelerated and the wrists extended as in the normal hitting position (Fig 51 (b) and (e)). The upper part of the body has had to open up earlier to allow the arms to come through. The right leg is bent to lower the body and ensure a good contact with the ball.

The body stays low and the stick follows the line of the ball (Fig 51 (c)). Maintaining balance in this final phase of the hit is essential (Fig 51 (f)). Slight variations in the movement of the hands, the position of the ball and the balance of the body can result in the ball being hit in the air or mishit.

The Slap Hit Fig 52

This is a useful skill when there is no time to slide the right hand up for a conventional hit (Fig 52 (a)). It is used over relatively short distances.

The ball is between the feet and the hands are apart in the normal pushing position. The weight is more to the right foot and the left shoulder faces the target.

The power in the hit comes from the transfer in weight and more particularly the action of the right arm, which punches through the ball (Fig 52 (b)).

Fig 52   The slap hit.

(a)

(b)

The left arm does little more than keep the stick on line. It can be used in many situations but is seen as a useful method of putting a rapid shot at goal in a rebound situation.

5

THE SKILL OF PASSING

This is such a central and fundamental facet of the game but is paradoxically rarely given the emphasis it requires if the standards are to be improved. Within the game there are a large number of factors which influence whether a pass will be successful or not, and because of this it is essential that players understand the basic principles that apply to passing as early as possible in their careers.

The principal objective of passing is to give the receiver the opportunity of performing another move to the advantage of the team in possession. Inherent in this basic principle is the concept that the passer does everything possible to make certain that the pass is given to the receiver, so that he will have the greatest opportunity to perform the next move. The other obvious but fundamental purpose of passing is to beat defenders either directly by forward passes beyond defenders or indirectly by cross-field passes, so that colleagues may beat defenders with forward movements of the ball.

The Components of Passing

The most crucial decision-maker on the field at any one time is the player in possession of the ball. Within the skill pattern of passing he *has control* over certain factors such as the speed at which he passes the

Fig 53   Sean Kerly looking for a pass against West Germany in the 1988 Olympic final.

ball, the direction in which he passes, the timing of the pass, the deception used to confuse the opposition, and the variety of the pass, which depends on the speed and direction of his own movement with the ball.

The player with the ball is also influenced by a number of factors that are *not directly within his control*, like the movement of his colleagues, the movement of the opposition, the surface on which play is taking place, and the area of the pitch in which he is positioned.

The area of the pitch is an important factor in that the greater the risk in the pass, the more important it is to make certain that if the pass fails, the opposition do not gain a disproportionate advantage. This is why passes with a high risk element should not be made in the defensive area of the field.

The basic concept of all passing is a very simple one: to pass a ball to the receiver so that he has the opportunity to perform the next move, be it a pass, a dribble or a shot. To allow this to happen the giver of the pass must make certain that the ball reaches the target, providing the receiver with sufficient time and space and therefore opportunity to succeed.

With the exception of shooting for goal, the objective of passing is to help the team achieve incisiveness through the opposition's defence. This can be the result of the speed of the pass, the speed of the player with the ball or receiving the ball and running with it, or the quality of the movement of a group of attackers to expose the defence.

Factors Influencing Successful Passing

While the position and movement of other players on the field, that is both colleagues and opposition, are crucial to the outcome of a passing movement, the most important areas of skill that require detailed attention are those related to the player in possession of the ball, that is the decision-maker. The responsibility of a successful pass lies primarily with this person. The responsibilities of the receiver will be dealt with later.

Although it is important to realize the interdependency of all the factors within the

Fig 54 Violet McBride passes in the Great Britain versus United States match in the 1988 Olympics.

control of the person with the ball, it is not difficult to set up practices that emphasize each particular aspect; in this way players can not only improve each area but will also learn to appreciate how the various facets fit together to improve the quality of the passing skills.

Speed of the Pass

This is obviously primarily related to the distance the ball has to travel to reach the target and the opportunities available for the opposition to intercept. In a congested area or where there is considerable distance between the striker and the potential interceptor, passes have to be given with greater pace. In these particular cases a slower pass can be given only if deception can be used to fool the opposition.

A fast pass to a fast-moving player can be very effective and incisive but it is a very difficult skill pattern to perform successfully. A slow pass to a slow-moving player, while it may be very safe, does not maximize the opportunity for any incisive movement, as the whole process will probably take too long to take advantage of poor opposition positioning. It must also be remembered that it is very difficult for a fast-moving player to make a pass at any great speed. There is always a need for the player to cut down the speed of running before he is able to make a pass of any power.

It is not difficult to set up practices which emphasize the speed of the pass and assist the players to assess when it is best to use passes that are given with greater or less pace.

The Target for the Pass

PASSES DIRECTLY TO A STICK
In this instance it is very rare

Fig 55   Richard Dodds (England) forces a pass away in spite of the attentions of the Pakistan centre forward during the 1986 World Cup.

that in a passing movement a ball is played to a player's stick while that player is completely stationary; usually he is moving and will continue to move after he receives the ball. It is important in these instances for the receiver of the pass to show the target to his colleague so that the player in possession of the ball is able to see exactly where his colleague requires the pass. In this way, the giver of the pass is able to assist the receiver in setting up the next movement. While it is preferable that the receiver should attempt to be going forward toward the opposition goal, as this makes it more difficult for the defenders, there are times when the receiver has to run across the field or even away from the opposition goal to receive passes on the stick.

Fig 56   Martyn Grimley passes against Australia in the 1988 Seoul Olympic semi-final.

PASSES INTO SPACE

The most telling passes into space are those made behind the defenders so that another attacker can move forward on to the ball. Because defenders are very wary of offering this space to forwards, it normally takes considerable deception to successfully make a pass into this space. A more common occurrence is that the ball is played forward into space and another attacking player moves across the field and collects the ball before turning to run forward. This kind of movement is not quite as incisive as when the player is already running forward into the space, as inevitably he has to slow down in order to change direction.

Learning how to successfully pass into space is not as difficult as it may initially appear. In fact, almost all passes to a moving player who is more than a few metres away are actually directed into a space for the receiver to move onto. It is not a large step in a player's mind to move from this concept to one in which the space is identified by both passer and receiver and the ball is put into that space for the latter to use. The attacker needs to have the defender at a considerable disadvantage (pace, deception, change of direction) to give maximum opportunity in these situations as the ball is free for some time.

The Timing of the Passing Movement

This aspect of passing is probably the most crucial and is dependent upon both the player in possession and the receiver. It is a factor intrinsic to all passing movements and yet it is difficult to isolate and explain.

Timing is best developed when players think more of the needs of their colleague than themselves; when they think more of the quality of the movement as a whole, rather than just their component. Passes are given so that the receiver has every opportunity to continue the movement. The receiver moves so that the passer has every chance to make a pass that will allow the passing movement to continue.

Passing movements that illustrate high-quality timing are a joy to behold; the whole movement flows with the many individual parts harmonizing into a continuous stream and the players at each stage appearing to have plenty of time and/or space in which to work. This is the ultimate

Fig 57 Warren Birmingham passing before Stephen Blöcher or Ekhart Schmidt can put in a tackle. World Cup, 1986.

Fig 58   Ekhart Schmidt showing his awareness of his Polish opponent who is closing in to tackle. World Cup, 1986, London.

situation that players and coaches are always seeking to achieve and as in all skills and strategies it needs to be developed progressively. To maintain high-quality passing movements under increasingly demanding circumstances (speed, space and competitive stress) requires attention to detail by both passer and receiver, along with an understanding of each other's needs in order to achieve the common goal.

The Variety of Pass

Because it is the responsibility of the person in possession of the ball to give the very best possible pass to the receiver, it is important that the player has a considerable repertoire of passes on which he can draw to suit the situation. While this is clearly closely related to deception, there are often cases within the game when a

defender responds in such a way as to demand that the attacker alters the kind of pass he was going to make if he wishes to be successful. For example, a defender may partly anticipate the line of the pass and look to intercept the ball with a horizontal stick close to the floor, thus demanding that if the pass is still to be successful, it has to be lifted over the low stick. There are a considerable number of subtle variations upon almost every pass that a player can give and it is important that players appreciate the effectiveness of these subtleties. This can only be done properly in the practice environment.

Deception

This is an essential weapon in the armoury of any player in possession of the ball, which is far too often greatly

underused. The deception does not have to be elaborate for it to be successful, as there is usually a need only to distract the attention of a defender or move him into a position to your advantage for a fraction of a second, which is usually long enough for you to take advantage of the situation with a pass. It must be remembered that deception is more difficult to perform the faster one is moving, not only because it is more demanding upon the player performing the deception, but also because for deception to be truly effective there needs to be a short time delay before the pass is made; the defender will otherwise not have reacted to the deception, so providing the opportunity for the pass to be successful.

The basic ploy in deception is to move or pretend to move in the direction opposite to where the pass is going to be made, but there are numerous variations that players can develop.

An important factor is that players recognize the deceptive skills of each other so that they then have the opportunity to anticipate where the pass is actually going to be made. Both the skill of deception and the understanding between players can only come through practice. It is quite easy to set up simple situations such as 2 vs 1 that allow players and coach to emphasize deception and promote greater understanding of how it can be achieved and how it can be best used within the team.

The following examples of practices for passing are analysed according to the Factors Influencing Successful Passing, to promote greater understanding in the players. No answers to the questions are given, simply because there may be several, and it should prove a good exercise for both coach and player to work out for himself.

Practices for Passing
There are innumerable practices that can be developed to improve the passing skills of players but whatever they are, they ought to cover one or more of the following situations that will always occur in the game.

1. Where the receiver is moving from left to right and ahead of the player in possession.
2. Where the receiver is moving from right to left and ahead of the player in possession.
3. Where the receiver is ahead but moving back toward the player in possession.
4. Where the receiver is moving forward and ahead of the player in possession, with the pass coming from the left.
5. Where the receiver is moving forward and ahead of the player in possession, with the pass coming from the right.
6. Where the receiver is moving alongside the player in possession.
7. Where the receiver is supporting the player in possession from behind.
8. Where the receiver is planning to give a first-time pass in return.
9. Where the receiver is moving closer to the player in possession.
10. Where the receiver is moving away from the player in possession.
11. Where the receiver is tightly marked.
12. Where the receiver is being closed down quickly by an opponent.

In addition to these examples, the passer and the receiver can be moving at various speeds. The result therefore is that there are an enormous number of variations that need to be mastered by a player in the skill of passing and there are a vast number of challenges that can be set to players within the practice environment to motivate them to work at this vital area of the game.

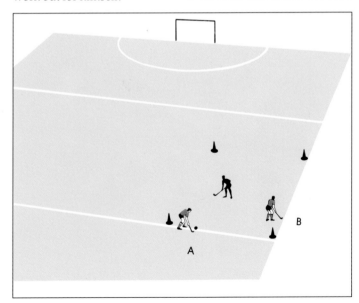

PRACTICE 1 Fig 59
In this game situation the two attackers are playing against the one defender. Player A has the ball and Player B is ahead of him and to his right moving forward with A. A moves forward with the ball and aims to pass to B, so that B can easily go beyond the defender.
Speed of the pass How does the speed of the pass influence the situation? Does the pass have to be faster the closer A gets to the defender?
The target for the pass Is the target stick or space? What happens to the target as A and B move forward? What is the outcome if the pass is directed behind the target?

Fig 59   Passing from left to right in a 2 vs 1 situation.

The timing of the passing movement   What is the advantage of an early pass? What can be the disadvantage of an early pass? Where ideally in relation to the defender would Player B like to receive the pass? What extra demands are put on the attackers if Player A delays his pass? Are there any advantages to him delaying the pass?

The variety of pass   What is the most obvious pass to be used by A? How might the kind of pass vary as A gets closer to the defender before passing? What are the cues for the player with the ball to decide the kind of pass?

Deception   If an early pass is made by A, is deception necessary? If it is, in which direction do the attacking players wish the defender to move? What kind of deception can be used as A gets closer to the defender?

PRACTICE 2
In this example the pass is still from left to right in a 2 vs 1 situation but Player A makes the pass with the reverse stick and Player B is supporting his colleague from behind or alongside and to his right.

Similar questions to the ones posed in Practice 1 within each area of work should be asked. Some of the answers may be different from those before. The kind of knowledge this promotes within players develops far greater understanding of the skill of passing.

It is not difficult to integrate these kinds of practices into more game-like situations by:

1.   Putting them into particular areas of the pitch.
2.   Increasing the competitiveness of the opposition and considering the

strategies that the defender may use.

This kind of work to develop greater understanding in the art of passing can be done for an endless number of situations that can be seen to occur in the game. The physical components of these skill patterns are very simple and it is therefore vital to continually challenge the players (according to their particular skill level) so that they are always learning. The relevance to the game situation needs ongoing appraisal by both coach and player if the maximum returns are to be gained. It may be advantageous to add a shot at goal or a further pass at the end of practices such as the examples above to allow the vehicle to be more realistic for players, while placing emphasis on the improvement

Fig 60   Ignacio Escude and Shabaz tussle for the ball during the 1988 Seoul Olympics.

in the understanding of the passing skill.

Although this section has really only scratched the surface of the skill of passing, it is hoped that it has set up the basic principles which will allow closer analysis of any passing pattern and provide a greater opportunity of gaining the kind of information necessary to improve players' performance. Almost every practice will include the skill of passing, therefore making it possible for a coach to set challenges that emphasize any particular aspect of this skill that he may perceive to be in need of improvement. For example:

1.   The smoothness of the whole passing movement between players.
2.   The timing of the passes in a square and through movement between two players.
3.   The way of utilizing the loop movement in 2 vs 1.

The Responsibilities of the Receiver

The role of those players without the ball is quite simply to make themselves available for a direct pass from the person in possession or to be ready to make themselves available for a pass from the next person likely to receive the ball. They are in effect doing everything they can to help the decision-maker. Clearly those people closer to the player in possession or more likely to receive a direct pass have a greater responsibility to provide this support.

Probably the most crucial aspect of the role of the receiver of a pass is the timing of any movement that player has to make in order to offer

the person in possession the opportunity of making a successful pass. All too often the receiver makes this movement with too little consideration of whether the timing is correct for the player in possession. In reality the receiver tends to make the movement when he wants to rather than when the man in possession needs him to. The recognition of a possible passing movement between players is normally made through eye to eye contact and while there can be no hard and fast rule on this, observation of players clearly shows that many errors are caused by the receiver making any necessary movement far too early, often long before the player in possession is ready or able to give the pass. There is thus a great deal of work to do in practices emphasizing the timing of the movement by the receiver, which must be based

upon the needs of the player in possession, and this aspect is closely linked to the skills of creating space and receiving the ball.

Receiving the Pass

This skill pattern is a combination of creating the opportunity to receive the pass and then controlling the ball. Each of these two components will be studied separately but, of course, in reality they need to be joined together to promote the understanding and improvement of the skill pattern.

Creating the Opportunity to Receive the Pass

As this is a move for the attacking players, a useful starting point is to consider what would be ideal from the defender's point of view. In the case of a defender marking

---

General Principles of Controlling the Ball

1.   The receiver's eyes and stick should be along the line of the ball for as long as possible and the receiver should watch the ball right on to the stick.
2.   The right hand is the key to the successful cushioning of the ball so that it can be repositioned as the receiver requires. This hand needs to be strong but able to make the stick 'give' at the moment of impact.
3.   The receiver should always try to be in a balanced position when controlling a pass. This can be done face on to the ball, with the body turned sideways to the line of the ball and even when the player is running, although of course the skill becomes more difficult the faster the player is moving.
4.   Looking for subsequent passes is an important part of a player's skill and this can be done before he receives a pass or after he has controlled it, not as he performs this vital skill.
5.   If a player wishes to control the ball and move in another direction quickly, then it is advantageous to be in a more upright position as it is much easier for the body to pivot.
6.   Controlling the ball with a horizontal stick is quite common on artificial turf and pitches. While this skill is particularly useful for intercepting passes made by the opposition and collecting poorly directed passes by one's colleagues, it does have limitations with regard to controlling the ball and moving off or changing direction quickly.

a potential receiver of a pass, it is much easier for that defending player when he is able to see both the attacker he is marking and the ball, or when any movement made by the attacker to reach a position in which to receive the pass is done in such a way as to give the defender sufficient time to react to the movement or even to anticipate it.

In order to create the opportunity to receive the pass, the attacking player must therefore move in such a way as to provide himself with both space and time. The timing of the movement into the space is therefore crucial, as is the ability to control the ball in that space before the defender is able to adequately respond to the situation. It is important to note that normally the receiver has to settle or certainly slow down when in the act of controlling the ball and this is why both time and space are required; a faster pass to the receiver who has settled can provide those extra milliseconds that he may need to get the ball under control, whereas a slower pass to a player who continues to move will allow that player to control the ball and continue moving into space away from the defender. Both these simple skills used at the right time can be extremely effective.

Having understood what a player is attempting to perform, it is relevant to consider what strategies he can use to create the opportunity to receive a pass. Almost all movements by players to create space and time for themselves are a combination of acceleration, change of direction and distraction.

ACCELERATION
This is one of the greatest assets in any team game and the player who is blessed with

Fig 61   Player B moves so that it is difficult for the defender to watch both him and his colleagues with the ball. The player with the ball runs at the marking defender. This may distract the defender so that the other attacker has the opportunity to find space alongside or beyond the defender.

this particular gift can in fact pay less attention to the other two strategies when he is attempting to create space. It also allows a player to accelerate away from a defender even when he is running and therefore gives him an extra dimension in this skill of creating space.

CHANGE OF DIRECTION
A sudden change of direction by a player can create the necessary time and space in which to receive a pass and, of

Fig 62   Netherlands versus Pakistan, 1984 Olympic games. Note how the defender is able to scan for passes while moving with the ball.

course, when coupled with acceleration it creates even more valuable time and space. If a player has considerable acceleration, then he may not need any other strategy in conjunction with the change of direction, but where the difference in acceleration between attacker and defender is much smaller then strategies such as getting the defender off balance become important. This can be achieved by forcing the defender to move in order to maintain a good defensive position. If the defender is being forced to move backward, the attacking player may well have the opportunity of changing direction quickly enough and at the right time to create valuable space. The more congested the situation is, for example around the attacking shooting circle, the more likely an attacker is to use this particular strategy. This strategy is often combined with that of distraction.

DISTRACTION
This strategy is based upon the principle of not allowing the defender the ideal situation. If the attacking player can move in such a way as to make it very difficult for the defender to see both him and the ball, provided that he is able to see his colleague with the ball and the defender, then he will have an advantage and probably be able to change direction or accelerate into space to receive the pass.

A second method of preventing the defender from having the ideal situation is for the player with the ball to dribble at a defender who is marking another attacker. This action may well attract the attention of the defender, allowing the second attacker to find the space and time required to receive the pass successfully (Fig 63).

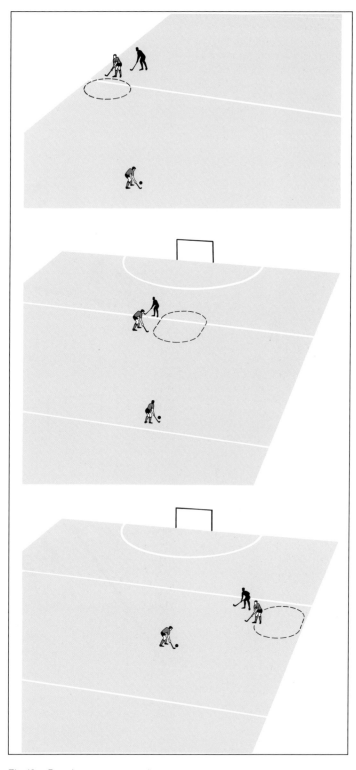

Fig 63   Creating space to receive a pass.

83

Fig 64   Creating space for a third person.

Obviously the success of these moves depends totally upon the timing of the movement of the receiver in conjunction with the pass from the player in possession. There are, however, some basic principles according to which the two players can work, so that through practice they increase their understanding of each other's skills and thereby the opportunity for success. In almost all of the situations it is the receiver who initiates the space-creating movement. It is vital that both players recognize the cues that trigger the particular movement and after eye-to-eye contact, these cues are likely to be either bodily movements or targets shown by the stick or hand.

In Fig 63 the attacker wishes to receive the ball in the space in the shaded area. What movements could the receiver perform that would put the defender at a disadvantage and create the time to utilize the space? Which particular movements are the cue(s) for the passer to release the ball? Would these alter if the distance between the attackers was greater? See Attacking Strategies: Creating More Space in a 2 vs 1 for further examples.

While Fig 63 illustrates a player creating time and space in order to receive the ball, there are many instances in the game when a player moves in order to create space for a colleague to utilize, as in Fig 64. This strategy may be used in conjunction with those above or separately. However, the basic principles are the same: not allowing the defender the ideal defending position, thereby forcing a positional response that the player can use to his advantage. This movement is particularly useful when the marking is tight.

When does the receiver

More Challenging Practices for Passing and Receiving

While it can be argued that every single practice in hockey has something to do with passing and receiving, the following approach emphasizes this aspect of coaching.

The following questions can be posed for the situations in Figs 63–64 to promote greater understanding amongst the players. These questions are not in order of priority although they do tend to follow a logical progression:

Who initiates the move?
How will that player move to put the defender at a disadvantage?
What are the cues to this movement that can be seen by the passer?
In what direction does the player move in order to receive the ball?
Where does the receiver want the ball to be placed?
When does the pass need to be made?
In what position does the receiver want to collect the pass in order to make it as difficult as possible for the defender?
Does it need to be to the open stick or the reverse stick?
Does the pass need to be fast?
What are the likely moves that the receiver will make after he controls the ball?

This may suggest going into considerable detail when practising passing and receiving. Although this may not be necessary with all age ranges and abilities of player, the more able performers should look at movements in this detail if they are to understand them properly. From this understanding, players are then able to recognize situations more easily and respond to one another more rapidly.

For each situation the above questions should help to decide how the receiver could best move so that the ball can be received in the shaded areas. The shaded areas in these practices are the areas players should seek to exploit. Although certainly not the only areas that one can exploit, they are the ones that given these circumstances tend to be used by players and therefore provide a realistic objective in practice.

The emphasis at first should be on the movement of the marked attacker and then the pass given by the player in possession. Remember, this is a practice for the attackers and therefore the defender should not be too competitive at first. It is all too easy in these situations for the defender to ruin the practice. As the attackers become more competent then the coach can allow the defender to become more competitive.

As players improve the emphasis can be shifted toward the movement that has to be made after control is successfully accomplished. Can the player in possession beat the defender and if so how? Can he pass back to his colleague? To introduce the skill of adding another movement to the sequence of creating space, entering the space and receiving the ball, it is sometimes useful to reduce the complexity and competitiveness until the movements are mastered and the players are more confident.

These practices also promote the ability of the passer to play the ball into space so that it arrives when the receiver needs it. Emphasis upon this timing of the pass is essential.

Fig 65   A Russian midfield player attempts to pass the ball past Stephen Batchelor and Kulbir Bhaura of England during the 1986 World Cup.

move into the space? What could the defender do if it is clear that the player creating the space is unable/unlikely to receive the ball? What lessons does this have for the attacker creating the space? What are the key factors going through the mind of the defender in this situation? Can this knowledge be used advantageously?

Controlling the Pass

Having successfully created the opportunity to receive the pass, the player then has to perform the skill of controlling the ball. While there are some simple basic principles that apply to almost every situation in which a player is controlling the ball, there are subtle variations in body position and movement according to where the ball has come from, the direction in which the receiver is moving and what he wishes to perform next. The last of these is far more important than players often consider. A player ought to know what skill he wishes to perform after he has received the ball and therefore he really must give himself every opportunity of being able to perform that next skill as soon as possible, be it a pass, a shot or a dribble. Perhaps the most fundamental factor with regard to controlling the ball is the quality of the pass that has been given to the receiver; while the ideal pass cannot always be provided, the closer the passer is able to get to this ideal, the greater the opportunity for the receiver.

Finding Further Solutions Figs 66 and 67

The following situations are designed to lead on from those orientated to creating space and timing the movement and pass in the sidebar, but if they are too advanced for players their complexity can be lessened by reducing the movement of the receiver. For each of the receiving positions in Fig 66 (a)–(d) and for each of the indicated lines of movement after the ball is controlled, the following questions can be considered:

Can the receiver prepare for the subsequent movement

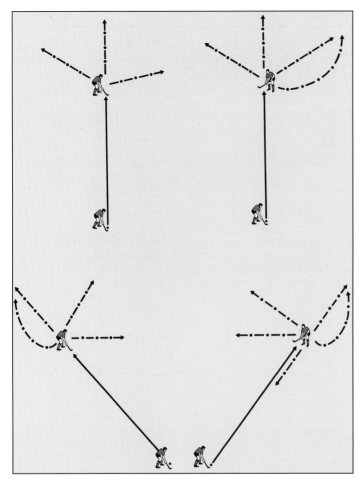

Fig 66 Creating space from different receiving positions.

All these questions (and others) can draw out many solutions to help solve the challenges and increase the understanding of the skills. To integrate these skills into a more game-like situation, a simple game can be played between three players in an area about 15m long and 10m wide (Fig 67). Players A and B are combining to try and beat the defender and take the ball over the end line (XY). A starts with the ball outside the box and no nearer the end line than 3m. This player cannot move with the ball or go into the box until B has received the pass. Once this is achieved, then the two attackers may play 2 vs 1 or B can beat the defender alone (no aerial play). The coach can vary the starting position of A to change the challenge, but the player should always be 3m back from the end line.

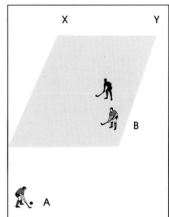

Fig 67 Integrating the passing skills in a more game-like situation.

prior to the ball being controlled?
What is the best movement of feet and body weight to accomplish the next move efficiently and quickly?
What stick movements are necessary?
How much does the body have to be slowed down to make certain the movement is successful?

Does the ball need to be received in slightly different positions to facilitate the subsequent moves?
Is it necessary for the receiver to move in another direction before adding the next movement, for example to give himself more room to manoeuvre?

6

GOAL SCORING

Games such as hockey and soccer are renowned for occasionally featuring outstanding goal scorers. These players are very sought after as they give a team an enormous advantage. Being feared by opponents for their ability to convert chances into goals, they increase the confidence of their team. However, the unique abilities of these performers seldom simply exist. While players such as Sean Kerly of Great Britain and Terry Walsh of Australia do have great goal-scoring abilities, one of the arts of coaching is not only to utilize these strengths but also to assist in their development. This provides players with opportunities to maximize their potential to the benefit of both themselves and the team.

There is a tendency within sport to search for and patiently await the arrival of a great player, whose appearance could instead be accelerated by sound coaching in the art of goal scoring. Naturally, not anyone can become a prolific goal scorer but it does provide a team with the opportunity of scoring goals without the availability of one of these rather rare performers, while also providing a pathway of developing and identifying goal-scoring talent. The outstanding goal scorer has a very good strike to success ratio but teams cannot rely upon one person to perform most of their goal scoring or to

await the arrival in their team of such a performer; it is far more beneficial if they have a number of players who are able to score goals and patterns of play and tactics that enhance their opportunities of doing so. The best-equipped teams not only have a player with outstanding goal-scoring abilities but also other players who are able to consistently score goals when given good opportunity. This combination allows the team to both put away the chances that they would expect and yet also score the occasional outstanding goal from a half chance.

If coaches are to understand the art of goal scoring more clearly in order to help players increase their skill in this area, then it is important for coaches and players to consider the basic principles and areas of study that relate to this skill.

These are how and where goals are scored, the role of the goalkeeper and the role of the defenders.

The Role of the Goalkeeper

It is useful for all players to understand what a goalkeeper is trying to achieve in a situation where an opponent has a goal-scoring opportunity, as they will be able to develop skills and tactics that enhance their opportunity to beat the goalkeeper.

The good goalkeeper will always try to dominate the situation and influence the way in which a player attempts to shoot at goal. He will prefer, of course, to make the player shoot from as far away from the goal as possible and from as narrow an angle as he can achieve. He will either attempt

---

How and When Goals are Scored

With the exception of direct shots from penalty corners a large proportion of goals scored are from within a 10m radius of the goal and usually achieved by the following:

1. An outstanding piece of individual skill finishing with a shot at goal.
2. Deflections at goal from a centre or pass from outside the circle.
3. A shot from a pass from a colleague within the circle.
4. A shot from a rebound from the goalkeeper or a defender's stick.

While not all goal-scoring opportunities are within 10m of the goal, it is important that some of the practices related to goal scoring incorporate the above skills, as clearly they are an important aspect of goal scoring.

to make the player rush the shot, thereby making an error, or try to delay the shot, so that he is able to smother the goal-scoring attempt or get into the best position to narrow the angle and make the save. Players should also remember that while a goalkeeper's legs are longer than his arms and therefore able to cover a wider range, they cannot move as quickly. This can have an important influence on the type of shot that a player makes in a goal-scoring situation.

A goalkeeper will always attempt to dominate the situation psychologically and physically, and players must be able to resist these pressures when making shots at goal. Ian Taylor had a unique ability to create a presence which had an adverse influence upon the performance of potential goal scorers. He was not only able to anticipate where shots were going to be made, but because of his skill in saving many shots that other goalkeepers would have missed, he psychologically forced potential scorers to go too close to the posts or to rush the shot, both of which tilted the scales towards the goalkeeper and his defence, thus winning the battle.

The Role of the Defenders

Defenders have very similar objectives to the goalkeeper when they are faced with the likelihood of a player having a shooting opportunity. They will force the shot to be made from the position that gives the attacker the least opportunity to score – from the edge of the circle, from as narrow an angle as possible or from a position in which he cannot get a telling shot at goal. They can also force the attacker to rush the shot by their physical presence. These objectives can be achieved by clever play by the defender or defenders, which is invariably assisted by forwards who do not make maximum use of the opportunity they have. All too often the attacking players assist the defence in one or more of the following ways:

Fig 68   Desperate clearance at the 1988 Seoul Olympics.

Fig 69　Imran Sherwani about to score Great Britain's first goal against West Germany in the 1988 Olympic final.

1.　The pass to the player who may shoot is telegraphed, thereby giving the defender the opportunity to intercept or negate the shot.

2.　The receiver moves too early into the space he wishes to use for the shooting opportunity or takes too long in preparing for the shot, thereby allowing the defender to cover the danger.

3.　Two attackers position themselves in the circle so that one defender can threaten a pass to either of them.

By understanding these factors which are uppermost in the defenders' minds, forwards will be much more successful in converting a potential goal-scoring opportunity into reality.

General Principles of Goal Scoring

The following general principles cover the factors already discussed relating to where goals are generally scored from and the objectives of the defenders as well as the accepted technical, tactical and psychological aspects important in goal scoring.

Technical

In order to make it as difficult as possible for the goalkeeper to get into the ideal position, it is important that attacking players are capable of propelling a shot at goal as quickly as possible after they have controlled the ball or entered the circle. They will then have a longer period of time during which to shoot effectively, and hopefully improve their chances of scoring, the goalkeeper not being able to exert as much pressure as he might have done. Achieving a good body position for an early strike at goal is a function of the combination of balance, strength and skill. It is more difficult for players to provide an effective strike at goal when they are moving very quickly, unless the shot is a deflection.

90

Thus there has to be a compromise between speed of movement and balance, but the stronger a player is in his body, the more able he is to provide himself with a relatively stable striking position when moving at greater speeds or striking the ball from a less than ideal body position (Fig 71). Strength in the forearms is also an important component in goal scoring, particularly when the strike has to be made quickly or from difficult body positions.

The combination of leg, body and arm strength will provide the forward with the ability to change direction suddenly within the circle and shoot from a wide range of angles and a variety of body positions.

The speed of a player is important in providing him with the opportunity of getting into a shooting position, while success within that shooting position is often dependent upon the player's ability to reduce the pace of his movement to provide him with the necessary balance for the shot. Coupled with the ability to get into a good shooting position and perform a variety of shots is the awareness of the player's position in relation to the goal. It is often said of a good goal scorer that he always knows where the goal is and is able to put a shot on target. This ability must not be underestimated or the practising of it neglected. The disadvantage of a quality goal-scoring forward is that occasionally he may strike for goal from a position which is very unlikely to lead to a score; however, this is so closely bound up with the psychological aspect of goal scoring that it is a small price to pay for the enormous benefits he may provide his team. It is important to encourage a goal scorer to keep shooting from all kinds of angles, while at the same time develop his ability to assess the situation quickly

Fig 70 Rek of West Germany goes for goal against the Netherlands in the bronze medal play-off game at the 1988 Seoul Olympics.

so that he will recognize when there is a person in a better position to shoot than he is, and use that person to the benefit of the team.

Psychological

It is impossible to create a simple model of a high-quality goal-scoring player but the following two psychological traits are common:

1.   Players have a high expectation of scoring at almost every attempt borne out of a positive and optimistic view of shooting.

2.   Their overwhelming desire and enjoyment of scoring goals manifests itself in a confidence and calmness in their performance, which enhances their ability to seize upon and convert goal-scoring chances.

Goal scoring is, without doubt, habit forming. Practices and the feedback given to players during the training for goal scoring must emphasize and reinforce these psychological aspects. There is a fine line between taking risks and clinically assessing whether a colleague is in a better goal-scoring position; players must be trusted and allowed to follow their judgement of the situation. Errors of judgement are bound to occur. However, if discussion between player and coach is positive and open, and goal-scoring training is done at match tempo in competitive situations, performers will have the opportunity of practising decision-making under pressure.

The very best goal scorers seldom consider their own safety or that of the defenders or goalkeeper in the competitive situation; their principal objective is to put the ball in the net. Injury is therefore always a distinct possibility.

Tactical

While the technical and psychological facets of goal scoring are without doubt of primary importance, a shrewd awareness of a number of tactical considerations can provide players with more and better opportunities to score goals.

1.   Forwards should consider whether it is an advantage to the defender if he can simultaneously see both the ball and the forward. If this is the case, then it is clear the forward should alter his movement before he positions himself to receive the pass and create the shooting opportunity. The kind of movement and its timing become very important elements in the creation of the space the player wishes to utilize for the goal-scoring opportunity. This space may be nearer the defender's goal than the defender himself, closer to the passer of the ball than the defender, or nearer the attacker's own goal than the defender. In all these situations, however, it is important that both the passer and the receiver are aware of the space they are seeking to exploit in order to harmonize their movements to the disadvantage of the defending team.

2.   The narrower the angle of the shot, the easier it is for the goalkeeper to make the target appear smaller and the more important it is for the forward to try and increase the percentages in his team's favour. To do this the most obvious is to make certain that the shot is on target; otherwise the forward should shoot towards the far post of the goal, which will provide colleagues with the opportunity of a deflection if there is any error, or the possibility of collecting the rebound for a second shot if the goalkeeper saves.

3.   A number of planned patterns of movement to help create shooting opportunities can only enhance a team's chances of goal scoring and these can quite easily be developed by utilizing much of

Fig 71   A goal-scoring opportunity for the USSR against India at the 1988 Olympic games.

the information already mentioned. The following six examples of right and left wing attacks and centres illustrating the areas of the circle that might be exploited for a goal-scoring opportunity, are taken from the game situation. However, these will always rely upon players getting into the appropriate positions and the passer being able to deliver the ball correctly. They will hopefully provide players and coaches with some basic patterns and perhaps even prompt ideas for interesting alternatives.

RIGHT WING CENTRES Fig 72
With defence running backwards Where the right wing has made an early centre with the defence running backwards, the right wing has probably beaten the left half and has been engaged by the next defender. This leaves the other central defender with the centre forward and the right half covering with the left wing. In the first instance the right wing is partly round the engaging defender and he passes the ball diagonally closer to the goal than the retreating defence (Fig 72). The centre forward is aiming to meet the ball before the engaged defender can intercept. This is achieved either by moving the defender towards the left of the goal early in the movement or by outpacing the defender by accelerating.

This is a relatively high-risk manœuvre as the ball is always going away from the centre forward.

From the base line outside the circle Sometimes it is necessary for the right wing to hit a centre from this position while moving relatively quickly. It is only possible for the player then to send a very flat centre towards the goal. As

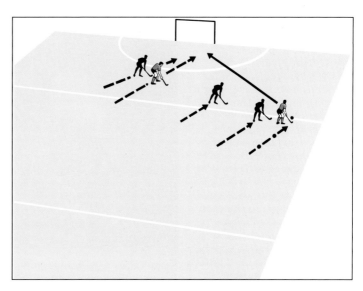

Fig 72   The right wing hits an early centre with the defence running backward.

defenders are likely to be quite close to the path of this pass it has to be played at considerable pace if there is to be any penetration. Likewise the centre forward and probably the left wing also have to be close to the line of the pass. Because it is difficult for the right wing in this situation to hit anything but a flat centre, the two leading strikers can commit themselves to the line of the centre, which is approximately 3–5m from the goal line, as this will be out of the goalkeeper's reach should it get as far as the goal before a player intercepts. Consider the possible alternatives to this kind of centre by the right wing, particularly if he is able to slow down his movement so that he has a greater range of pass or if he obtains a free hit from a defender. Which players could offer an alternative position for a pass and where would this pass be best placed?
Cutting in towards the goal
Where the right wing is either cutting in from the right

diagonally towards the base line or is moving along the base line towards the goal, because of his position, it is possible to make passes through a wider arc than in the previous example, and other areas of the circle become possible target areas for passes that may lead to goal-scoring opportunities.

Firstly, the area in front of and to the right of the right-hand post 5–7m from the goal is ideal for the centre forward to look for a pass from which he may try a quick shot.

Secondly, it is possible to utilize the area near the top of the circle at almost right angles to the base line and point where the wing is in possession of the ball, as the defenders will be moving backward towards their own goal and will wish to cover the most dangerous area, approximately a 10m radius from the goal. While the path back towards the inside right position provides the defence with the opportunity to force the attackers to shoot from the edge of the circle and, hopefully, give themselves time to pressure the shot, the attackers can create considerable problems for the defending team if they perform the skill effectively. The defenders will have to change direction to close in on the player now in possession and the attacking centre forward and the left wing will be able to position themselves to collect rebounds from the goalkeeper. It is important in this situation that the receiver of the pass does not enter the circle too early, otherwise by the time he has collected the ball and put it into the shooting position, he may find that he is already 2m inside the circle and therefore more vulnerable to nearby defenders.

Finally, if the left wing does not go close to the goal when the right wing is in this position, he has the advantage of utilizing the back of the circle in the inside left position. While the right wing may find it more difficult to find the left wing positioned in the inside left area, a hard strike can often provide the opportunity for the left wing to control the ball and make an effective shot at goal. The right half will almost certainly automatically cover the area in front of the goal.

LEFT WING CENTRES
From just inside the 25 yard line   Some left wings are able to make an early centre from the 25 yard line while running forward. Excellent movement of the feet around the ball is necessary in order to make the left to right hit; in some exceptional circumstances players use a reverse stick hit. Consider the areas toward which this centre can be effectively made and the positioning and movement of the centre forward in order to make maximum use of such

Fig 73   Rick Charlesworth cuts through the Great Britain defence in the 1988 Olympic semifinal (Great Britain won 3–2).

centres. If the left wing is slowed down or stopped by good defensive play from the right half or a covering defender, what alternative move could he and the centre forward make if they were seeking to maintain the advantage that they had?
From near the base line
These centres are invariably slower to execute than those by the right wing as they nearly always require that the left wing pulls the ball back away from the base line, so that he is able to turn his body to strike the ball from left to right. Bearing this in mind, which area of the circle could the left wing utilize in order to make a telling pass that could result in a goal-scoring opportunity?
From the base line inside the circle   In this situation the left wing is either cutting diagonally toward the base line or moving along the base line. These two situations will vary in the following aspects: the way the ball is likely to be carried by the attacker and therefore the opportunities of seeing a pass to any of the supporting players; the ability

of the forward to make a hard pass through a congested area; and the areas of the circle that could be most effectively used by other attacking players.

There are no completely right and wrong solutions to the challenges of creating patterns of play in order to convert centres into goal-scoring opportunities, although there are a number of possibilities that in the light of experience have proved more likely to succeed than others. The best solutions are found by considering the likely patterns of play of the defenders in these pressurized situations and the attacking attributes of the offensive team. Whatever solutions are chosen, it is important that they are practised and understood by all the players concerned as the timing of these situations is crucial and there is not a great margin for error for the attacking team.

The greatest frustration for the whole team is to see good attacking movements wasted through careless play in the final phase.

Fig 74   Kerly shoots against South Korea at the 1988 Olympics.

Goal-Scoring Skills

Balance is an essential ingredient of all goal-scoring skills. The best strikers are strong in the legs; so that even when they are not in the ideal position they can provide themselves with a relatively stable platform. It is also an advantage to have strong forearms, so that the ball can be propelled at goal using any of the following skills quickly and with power.

Hitting the Ball

If the player is moving forward with the ball prior to striking the ball at goal, then it is important that the body position is changed quickly to the striking situation. In Fig 50 notice how the body position is such that the left shoulder faces the target, the left foot is in line with the ball and the legs are slightly bent in order to provide a solid foundation. The arms accelerate the head of the stick through the ball, although the forward momentum of the body and transference of weight on to the front foot assist in generating the speed of the stick head. The head is kept steady throughout the movement and the eyes remain focused on the ball and do not look up to follow the path of the ball until after it has been struck.

There are times when it is not possible for the player to position the body ideally and sometimes it is necessary to strike the ball while off balance. Where the strike is being made with the weight on the right foot, while this is less than ideal, the right leg should be slightly bent to lower the body into the striking position and provide as solid a foundation as possible in the circumstances. The player turns his body as much as is possible to a sideways position, adjusting the movement of his hands during the striking phase to help him put the ball on target. These subtle adjustments can be refined only through practice and feedback from the coach to the player. If the receiver has to control the ball prior to striking for goal, then the quality of the first touch in this receiving skill is vitally important. Not only should the receiver control the ball, but he should also reposition it so that the strike can be made without delay while taking into account the positioning of the defenders. This skill is more difficult than moving the ball forward and into the striking situation and must therefore be continually practised. Much of its success relies upon the quality of pass given to the striker as well as the striker's skill in repositioning and striking the ball.

Chip Shot

With subtle variations in the movement of hands and feet in relation to the ball and of the path of the stick, chip shots can be played to beat the sliding goalkeeper or deliberately play the ball into the upper part of the net. In order to cause the ball to lift, the wrists are broken much earlier in the backswing, producing a steeper downswing of the stick. The hands at the point of impact tend to be behind the ball and the stick chops underneath the ball.

Slap Shot

This shot is played with the hands apart but it is a clear hit rather than a flick or a push. The advantage of this shot is that it can be played with control without quite as much preparation as an ordinary hit, yet it can be powerful. It does, however, demand sound technique as the body has to be in a stooped position. It is often used by forwards as a rebound shot or when the ball is moving slowly and they have to put in a strike at goal as quickly as possible although it is applicable to all players.

95

Flicks at Goal

These are probably less powerful than any of the striking skills in terms of goal scoring but they do provide a forward with a method of getting a shot on target quickly. They can be performed at the end of a dribbling skill, or very quickly after the ball has been controlled either from a pass or a rebound from the goalkeeper or a defender. A slight variation in these skills can be used to flick or lob the ball over a defensive goalkeeper.

Flicks and slap shots are most commonly used in the rebound situation. In performing these skills, it is important that the players are well balanced and make the correct decision as to whether to control the ball before they strike the ball toward goal or play the ball as it rebounds. If the ball is coming quickly toward them on the rebound, it is safer to control the ball before making a shot, although this, of course, will take a slightly longer time to perform. The most important aspect is to keep calm and controlled so that the player gives himself every opportunity of making good contact with the ball. In order to become accomplished in these situations, it is vital that meaningful practices are set up by the coach. This will necessitate understanding both how and where the ball is likely to rebound in both open play and at set pieces such as penalty corners.

Practices for Goal Scoring

All the following areas need to be emphasized in practices. Then they can be altered using the concepts fully explained under Planning Progressive Practices on page 25.

1. The techniques of the various shots.
2. The speed of control and then shooting.
3. The accuracy of the shot.
4. A positive attitude toward shooting and scoring.
5. Taking snap shots.
6. Being able to seize on secondary shots.
7. Exploiting various areas in the circle at the end of a passing movement.
8. Fast attacking moves followed by composure in order to put a good shot in at goal.
9. Choosing the correct shot for varying situations.
10. Shots available at set piece situations in attack.

Within all these areas of work there are a vast number of practices that can be set up and modified according to the skill and experience of players and the objectives set by the coach. Goal scoring is a vital part of the game and one that can easily be neglected. It is useful to try and finish every practice with a shot at goal even though the main aim of the practice may be to develop another skill or tactical area. Everyone likes to score goals and if it is possible to increase the confidence of all players in the goal-scoring situation then the team's likelihood of turning opportunities into goals must be enhanced.

Deflections

These shots at goal normally occur from a centre and, while the margin for error is not great, they can be extremely effective methods of scoring. On artificial turf pitches the smoothness of the surface allows players to lay the stick almost horizontal, thus increasing the opportunity to successfully achieve a deflection at goal. While it is possible to deflect the ball in a wide arc, most shots of this kind deflect from the stick at an angle greater than 90 degrees. Deflections from centres from the wing are therefore best made along the line of the near post or even outside of it. The distance a forward can cover when making a deflected shot is increased by him diving, and the combination of the smoother artificial turf and the ability to lay the stick horizontal has meant an increased number of these kinds of goal attempts, particularly on water-based artificial pitches.

Practising deflections on both forehand and reverse stick from centres promotes confidence in players in goal scoring.

7

BEATING A PLAYER

When beating a player the clear objective is to finish the movement with ball under control and goalside of the opponent. This can be achieved through passing the ball around the opponent or by dribbling the ball past the opponent. While the former method is often the safest and preferred, there is no doubt that dribbling round an opponent is an important skill pattern in the game. The factors that influence a player's decision to dribble around an opponent rather than pass the ball around him, or vice versa, can be grouped under a single simple heading, that is the recognition by the attacker that the defender is at a disadvantage. This disadvantage may manifest itself in one or more of the following:

1. The defender is out of position.
2. The defender is off balance and cannot react quickly enough to the movement of the attacker.
3. The defender is slower than the attacker.
4. The defender is less skilled than the attacker.
5. The defender has to cope with two or more attackers in his area.

If attacking players can recognize when defenders are at a disadvantage, it will be easier to decide whether to pass or dribble. But attacking players should not only react to the situation when the

---

Preferences of the Defenders
1. To gain time and the opportunity for other defenders to assist them by slowing down the attacking movement.
2. To close in on a slow or stationary attacker.
3. To be moved sideways by attackers rather than backward.
4. To force the ball away from the goal either backward or sideways.
5. To defend small or congested areas rather than larger or less congested areas.
6. In the majority of cases to have the attackers and the ball in front of them rather than behind them.

---

defender is at a disadvantage, but should also be more pro-active; that is try and manœuvre the situation such that the defender is put at a disadvantage rather than react to the situation only when he is at a disadvantage. To achieve this kind of development within attacking play, the players need to appreciate not only what they are trying to achieve but also the preferences and objectives of the defender. This knowledge will enable coaches and attacking players to formulate their strategies and improve their opportunities of putting the defenders at a disadvantage. Every situation is slightly different and demands from the defender an assessment of what is the least dangerous alternative that he would like the forwards to take.

These preferences and the priority defenders give to them will alter according to the situation and their position on the pitch. If the attacking players are aware of these changes then they are able to make adjustments to their play

and retain and exploit the advantages they have.

Strategies for Beating a Player

Having outlined some general principles which can be used to increase the amount of information available to attackers when they are faced with the challenge of beating an opponent, some of the strategies that can be used to achieve this objective will now be discussed. This section can be split up into three areas: common principles, preliminary work and skill patterns.

Common Principles

Pattern of movement There is a pattern in each of the strategies that will give the player every opportunity to succeed, and although the pattern is likely to alter slightly according to the situation, it is important for players to recognize and practise the patterns.

97

Fig 75   Karen Brown (Great Britain) beats a South Korean defender at the 1988 Seoul Olympics.

Technical movements   Each skill pattern will require particular movements of stick, ball and body and while there are again variations both according to the situation and between individuals, there are common principles which must be understood by players.

Timing of the movement

This is one of the most difficult aspects of beating a player to coach. The key factor is to help the attacker recognize the point in time when the defender has committed himself to a particular course of action that offers the attacker an advantage. While this can be gained only through experience, it can be improved if emphasized during a practice situation.

Speed of movement   The speed at which the player is moving with the ball has an influence upon the skills that can be performed. Intricate skills are far more difficult to perform successfully if the player is moving at high speed. It is important to encourage the player in possession to move at a speed which allows him to create or retain the advantage over the defender while at the same time providing him with the opportunity to perform the skills he wishes to convert the advantage into successfully beating the player. The term 'poise' is often used by coaches to describe this equilibrium to players. It will, of course, vary greatly between one player and another for the same skill performance.

Simplicity   This factor is clearly related to the previous one in that the faster the player is moving the simpler the technical skill should be (and probably needs to be) to ensure success. Simplicity also helps a player's colleagues when they are supporting the movement and anticipating the possible patterns of play.

Preliminary Work

This relates to the period of time when the player in possession recognizes or creates the disadvantage of the defender. In the former case the attackers will be looking to find a skill pattern that will exploit the situation while in the latter, the player in possession will probably seek to move and/or deceive the defender.

In moving the defender, the attacker may wish to take the defender to one side so that by changing direction quickly, the attacker can make use of the space that has been created or force the defender to move backward. This is a much more difficult skill for the defender and therefore gives the attacker greater opportunity to succeed. The movement of the defender by the attacker may also force the defender into an attempted tackle which again may provide the player in possession with the opportunity to beat the defender. In addition to moving the defender, the attacker may also use some kind of deception to increase the defender's disadvantage and the attacker's opportunity for success.

Skill Patterns

Several examples of beating a player are shown in Chapter 4 under Dragging the Ball (page 57). These can be re-examined, applying the questions in the

Preliminary Work

It is crucial in preliminary work to recognize the moment when the defender is most vulnerable and to respond accordingly. This demands considerable awareness by the attacking player and detailed analysis by the coach so that every assistance can be given to the player. For example, if an attacker is moving from right to left with the ball, with the aim of drawing the defender across the field so that he can then change direction and attack the space down the reverse stick side of the defender, then he should ask himself the following questions:

How fast do I move with the ball?
Where do I carry the ball?
How far away from the defender do I need to be?
What position do I want the defender to be in so that I can exploit the reverse stick side?
When do I change direction?
Where do I move with the ball on changing direction to give myself maximum opportunity to succeed?
What is the best foot pattern to use to change direction quickly and efficiently?
What cue might make me use deception and find another solution to the problem?

These questions may appear endless when developing skill patterns but the most important factor is for the players to be aware of them and learn from experience in both the practice and game situations.

Fig 76   Synchronized hockey. Parleveit (Netherlands) and Hannel (West Germany) drive for the ball.

sidebar on Preliminary Work to the situations.

An attacker may also learn to lift the ball over the outstretched horizontal stick of the defender on both the open and reverse side. What modifications to movement and technique might the attacker have to make?

Many attackers beat a defender by pushing the ball close to the feet and past the player. What does the attacker attempt to do in the preparation phase to make this more likely to succeed?

RUNNING WITH THE BALL AT SPEED

Where a defender has been put at a disadvantage and there is a clear opportunity to run with the ball at speed to beat him, then some of the more intricate skills described under Dragging the Ball on page 57 are unnecessary. Generally, players cannot run at maximum speed and keep the ball under close control, particularly when using the Indian dribble, but of course the closer a player can get to his maximum running speed and still be in control of the ball then the greater attacking opportunities he is likely to create. It is therefore important to practise running with the ball under control at speed.

On the forehand side   On this side of the body the ball needs to be slightly to the right and ahead of the body so that there is minimum restriction to the running movement of the legs; the body is in only a slightly stooped position. Certain players, particularly right wings, hold the stick in the right hand only when they have a clear run with the ball as this allows them to carry the ball further to the right and away from any opponents, and also in a less stooped position, thereby allowing them to be in a better running position. A weakness of this is that fine manipulation of the ball is limited and adjustments have to be made before any other skills can be performed.

On the reverse side   Players running through space with the ball to the left of the body very often make use of the left hand only on the stick and place the ball ahead and to the left-hand side of the body.

8
DEFENDING SKILLS

As the opposition gain possession of the ball, members of the team must reorientate to take up defensive responsibilities. The principal objectives are to delay any incisive/penetrative movement, and to regain possession.

The achievement of these two objectives depends upon the skilful performance of a number of basic defensive skills including marking, covering, closing down, channelling and tackling.

It is important to note that while each skill will be considered separately, they are, of course, interrelated and interdependent.

Marking

Marking is positioning yourself close to an opponent so that the player is unable to receive a pass; or having received the pass, can be tackled or harassed into making an error.

The actual position of the marker in relation to the opponent will vary according to:

1.   The area of the pitch.
2.   The distribution of both opponents and colleagues.
3.   The closeness of the player in possession to the player being marked.
4.   The likelihood of the player receiving a direct pass.
5.   The other duties demanded of the defender by the situation.

Defensive Principles

Underpinning all defensive work are a number of basic defensive principles, that is the defender should delay the opposition's movements; there should always be depth in defence; and the defender should understand the options open to the attackers in all situations.

Quality defensive play is developed more rapidly when players illustrate the important attributes of restraint, control and concentration.

Delay in defence can be achieved in a number of ways, including:
1.   Blocking the path of penetrative passes.
2.   Marking a player tightly to threaten a penetrative pass.
3.   Forcing a player to pass to a less dangerous area or one covered by other defenders.
4.   Engaging the player so that they cannot look for passes.

Depth is achieved primarily via marking or covering. The important aspect is to make certain that the defence is not too shallow and thereby vulnerable to penetration.

Understanding comes from studying the game, observing players and discussing skills and strategies with the coach and fellow players. It is accumulated over time both from matches and practice sessions.

Fig 77   The marking right half is well positioned between the attacker and the defending team's goal.

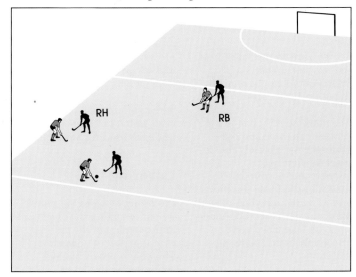

Fig 78   Marcello Giraffo (Argentina) attempts to intercept a clearance from a New Zealand player. World Cup, London, 1986.

In many situations, it is advantageous to be positioned as a marker so that:

1.   You are between the attacker and your goal.
2.   You can see both the ball and the attacker you are marking.
3.   You are on the ball side of the attacker so that interceptions can be made if the opportunity arises.

The marking right half in Fig 77 achieves all three of these while the right back is able to meet the first two.

There are, of course, exceptions to these situations and in particular when players mark ahead of their opponent. This can take place very effectively in the following situations:

1.   At free hits where the distribution of the defending side is well planned, allowing one or two markers to take the risk.
2.   In congested situations and/or where interceptions are of a high priority (e.g. free hits near the defending circle).
3.   When the play is contained in a narrow channel (e.g. close to the touch line).

Some of these possibilities will be examined in more detail under Defending Strategies.

Covering

Providing cover to the player who is engaging the opponent in possession of the ball is an essential part of defending. This role is nearly always combined with that of marking, and achieving the appropriate balance is very important. Within the act of providing cover a player is almost always blocking the route of a penetrative pass. This delays the opposition or offers them the opportunity of a less dangerous option. Inadequate or inappropriate cover will make the defender engaging the player in possession more vulnerable, demanding greater caution and delay, which will reduce the opportunity to regain possession.

Likewise, poor marking of players will have an influence upon the quality of the cover given to that marker. A covering defender cannot achieve the appropriate balance between marking and covering if fellow defenders are not performing their role effectively.

Fig 79   Closing down.

(a)

(b)

(c)

(d)

In the game situation players will be beaten and the skill of the covering defenders is to delay the attacking movement until effective cover can be re-established.

Closing Down Fig 79

This, at its simplest, is the movement of a player to engage the opponent receiving the ball (denying space). It is inextricably bound up with the other defensive skills and is worth looking at in detail as there are important decision-making and movement principles that are relevant to all the defending skills.

As the opponent is receiving a pass the defender engaging this player ought to have

processed or be processing a number of questions that will influence how he closes down and delays the player:

Can I intercept the pass?
Is there an incisive pass I must protect against?
How close should I (can I) go? This will depend upon the quality of the pass; the quality of the control; the support available to the attacker and the defender.
Can I stop forward movement?
Can I force the attacker's attention to the ball rather than passes?
Do I need to channel the player in a direction before I can exert more pressure?
Can I (do I want to) force the attacker onto my forehand stick?

The answers to these and other questions will influence the movement of the defender and needs to be understood and practised individually and in small groups.

Fig 79 illustrates a very simple example of closing down with no complicating factors for the defender such as other attackers to influence the situation.

The objectives of the defender in this case are straightforward:

1.   To stop/delay forward movement of the player with the ball.
2.   To force the attacker's attention to the ball by his presence.
3.   To be in a position to influence the actions of the

Fig 80   Two Australians close in for the tackle in the Australia versus South Korea match in the 1988 Olympics.

attacker and/or to respond effectively to any movement.
4.   To regain possession of the ball.

While regaining possession is, of course, the ultimate objective, it usually happens when the other objectives have been achieved. In many cases in the match situation, possession is regained by defenders other than the one engaging the attacker (e.g. interception of a subsequent pass). For this reason it is not essential when practising closing down to emphasize the tackling aspect. Closing down buys *time* for the defence and this in turn provides *opportunity* to regain possession.

Channelling

This is the result of clever positioning by defenders to dictate or restrict the movement of the attackers and/or the ball. It is primarily achieved during the marking, covering and closing down phases to direct the opposition into areas that are:

Closing Down

The following questions for Fig 79 will enhance understanding of the physical aspects of closing down and their relevance to other defensive skills.

Would the defender be moving at his fastest early or late in the movement?

When would deceleration occur? What is the cue?

How would the foot pattern alter?

How close does the defender have to be to start to pressure and influence the attacker?

What are the body shape and position of the defender as the attacker is approached?

What illustrates the ability to move quickly and in balance?

What are the advantages of the stick and hand position?

How is the defender influencing the movement of the attacker?

Has the defender delayed the attacker?

Are the attacker's options limited?

How long has the whole movement lasted?

Fig 81   Sean Kerly closes down on a Canadian defender in the 1984 Olympics (Great Britain won 3–0).

1.   Less dangerous for the defence (e.g. away from goal).
2.   More congested with defenders and are therefore traps (e.g. onto a free defender).
3.   More easily defended (e.g. close to the side line).

Fig 82   David Faulkner intercepts on the reverse stick.

Intercepting

This is the best method of regaining possession as it frequently allows the receiver the opportunity to move the ball forward quickly and incisively. Intercepting can be improved considerably through the clever combination of high-quality control of the ball along with individual and group defending. The very best interceptors recognise how large a gap they can leave and still intercept the passes. This requires practice before it can be utilized as a strategy.

Tackling

The ultimate objective of a defending team is to work together so that the opposition

105

Fig 83 The right-handed forehand stick tackle (Pleshakov, USSR) is used frequently on defenders who try and drag the ball from right to left.

Fig 84 Alison Ramsay attempting a reverse stick tackle. Great Britain versus South Korea, 1988 Olympic games.

106

are forced into a manœuvre that results in one of the following:

1. An error that cedes possession.
2. An interception of a pass.
3. A successful tackle of a player in possession.

The 'working together' aspect for defending includes closing down, channelling, marking and covering in addition to tackling. These will be considered together in the next chapter on Skill Patterns. At present the primary emphasis will be upon the technical aspects of tackling.

The actual tackle is the final action in a series of movements. These movements are related to a number of intermediate objectives or stepping stones. The defender will gain an advantage over the attacking player if he is able to move him in a preferred direction, limit his options, or deceive him as to the defender's action.

The achievement of these objectives which give opportunity to tackle successfully are influenced by the quality of the defender's preparation. In order to tackle effectively and consistently players must understand the influence and importance of a number of factors. These include footwork, balance, body position, stick position and hand position.

There are common principles related to each of these factors that are applicable to all types of tackle.

The Principal Coaching Points Related to Tackling

1. The defender must watch the ball and not be caught out by feints with the stick and body.

Footwork, Balance and Body Position

These three factors are so interrelated that it is pertinent to look at them together.

Footwork is perhaps the most important aspect of tackling that is inadequately emphasized during practice. It is fundamental to maintaining good balance and the appropriate body position during both the preparation and the actual tackle. Because most tackling is performed as a result of manœuvring an opponent who has possession of the ball, the following three aspects are essential:

1. To use relatively small steps so that the defender can rapidly adjust his positioning in response to the movements of the attacker, hopefully without losing any advantage he had gained.
2. Players must keep their body weight distributed to the front of their feet (the toes) rather than the heels, for as soon as the weight is on the heels they will not be able to readjust their position quickly and effectively.
3. Feet should be positioned in such a way that the player is able to move easily in almost any direction in response to the attacker. This is not easily achieved when the defender's feet are square to the line of movement of the attacker. While it is not impossible to tackle in this position, there are distinct disadvantages if this is the normal stance of a player when defending.

Good balance is imperative if the defender is to manipulate the attacker into a position/situation in which he can dispossess him. Maintaining good balance is achieved by lowering the centre of gravity and adopting a compact body shape without inhibiting fluid movement. This quality is best illustrated by Fig 79 on page 103.

In addition to the shape of the body facilitating good balance, the position of the defender in relation to the movement of the attacker is also an important factor. The defender can guide the attacker in a particular direction, limit his available options and increase the psychological pressure on him by intelligent positioning of the body. When studying the photographic sequences in Fig 79 this aspect should be considered not only in relation to the particular example, but also with respect to other similar situations that are recognized in the game.

2. He must use clever stick positioning, movement and feints to influence the actions of the attacker.
3. The work of the legs is essential. Nimble footwork and good balance are prerequisites for good tackling.
4. The defender must not run backward but turn his body and run alongside the attacker.
5. Good body positioning can influence the direction of the movement of the attacker.
6. The defender should delay the tackle until the best

possible moment.
7. The timing of the tackle should be disguised.
8. The defender must dominate the attacker both physically and psychologically.
9. He must understand the attacker's options.

THE JAB TACKLE Fig 85
From a position with both hands on the stick, the left arm pushes the head of the stick towards the ball (Fig 85 (a)). The left leg is stepping forward with the right leg beginning to

107

provide the driving force to push the body weight through the line of the tackle.

The point of contact is near the base of the ball, forcing it forward and upward away from the attacker (Fig 85 (b)). The left arm has extended, accelerating the head of the stick, and the right leg has pushed the body weight along the line of the tackle.

The stick and body follow the ball so that the defender can gain possession of the ball and set up an attacking opportunity (Fig 85 (c)).

This type of tackle can be used from the side to force a player to lose control. Even when tackling back on a player, a jab tackle can be used to push the ball out of the player's control.

Fig 85   The jab tackle.

(a)

Fig 86   Norman Hughes looks to jab tackle the ball away from the Dutch opponent during England's 1–0 win in the 1986 World Cup.

108

(b)

(c)

Fig 87   Elspeth Clemence making a jab tackle in the
Australia versus South Korea match at the Seoul Olympics.

THE OPEN STICK BLOCK TACKLE Fig 88

The attacker is being guided to the defender's open stick side by the body position of the defender. The right foot of the defender is almost in line with the right foot of the attacker (Figs 88 (a) and (b)). The defender is moving with the attacker so that he can decide when to make the tackle. The steps are small, both hands are on the stick and the body is in balance. The focus is on the ball.

As the tackle is made the body weight shifts forward over the left leg (Fig 88 (c)). Both hands are on the stick and apart, providing strength to the tackle. The head of the stick is low and the hands drop the handle of the stick to ground level at the last moment to provide the block. In this particular case the stick is positioned so that an area on either side of the ball is protected, thus making it

109

Fig 88   The open stick block tackle.

(a)

(b)

(c)

(d)

difficult for the attacker to avoid the block.

The speed of the attacker takes him beyond the defender while the forward movement into the tackle pushes the ball away from the attacker and gives the defender the opportunity to set up a counter attack (Fig 88 (d)).

THE REVERSE STICK BLOCK TACKLE Fig 92
The defender shadows the attacker in a well-balanced position, preparing to respond

Fig 89   Sergio Vigil of Argentina wins the tackle against New Zealand (World Cup 1986).

Fig 90   Richard Leman tackles Ekhart Schmidt in the 1988 Olympic final.

Fig 91   Volter Fried attempts to tackle Mark Precious in the 1984 Olympic semi final (West Germany won 1–0).

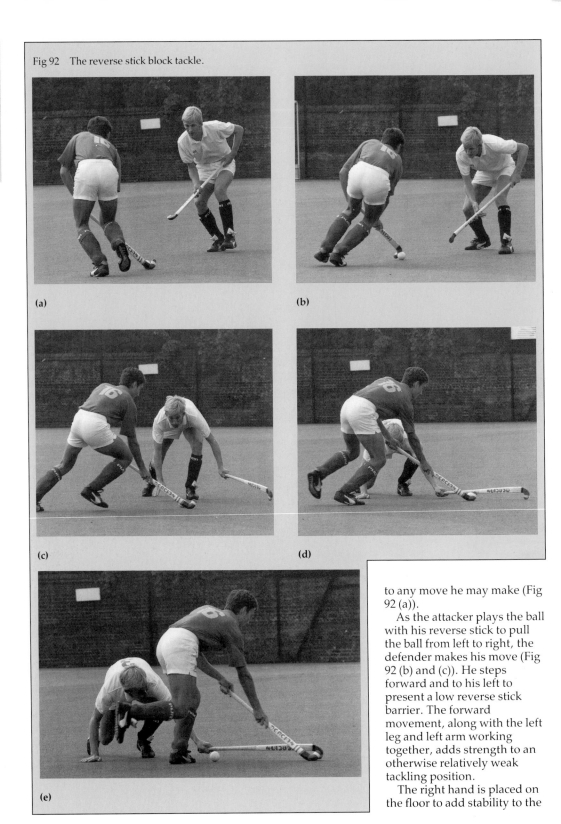

Fig 92 The reverse stick block tackle.

(a)

(b)

(c)

(d)

(e)

to any move he may make (Fig 92 (a)).

As the attacker plays the ball with his reverse stick to pull the ball from left to right, the defender makes his move (Fig 92 (b) and (c)). He steps forward and to his left to present a low reverse stick barrier. The forward movement, along with the left leg and left arm working together, adds strength to an otherwise relatively weak tackling position.

The right hand is placed on the floor to add stability to the

Fig 93   David Faulkner of England goes for a reverse stick tackle against a Russian player in the 1986 World Cup.

body. At the point of contact the left arm must be tense to withstand the force of the attacker's forward momentum (Fig 92 (d) and (e)). The head of the stick is on the ground and the left hand is on or very close to the ground to produce the widest possible barrier. The momentum of the attacker usually causes him to overrun the ball and lose possession.

THE REVERSE STICK UPRIGHT TACKLE Fig 96
This is probably the most difficult tackle to perform successfully, particularly while retaining two hands on the stick. In match situations most of these tackles are made with only the left hand on the stick but the basic principles illustrated in the photographic sequence still apply.

The defender is goalside of the attacker and infield,

Fig 94   A pincer movement. Pleshakov of the USSR makes a neat reverse stick tackle on the Dutch midfield at the 1986 World Cup.

113

Fig 95 Caes Deepevein (Netherlands) attempts a reverse stick tackle against a Pakistan player in the 1984 Olympics.

positioning himself so that he is restricting the options of the attacker (Fig 96 (a)). The defender accepts that he cannot stop the attacker from trying to exploit the channel on his reverse stick side (Fig 96 (b)).

The defender has run with the attacker, trying to cause him to lose control of the ball sufficiently to allow a tackle to be made (Fig 96 (c)). The stick protects his feet while inviting the attacker to continue forward. The body position allows the defender to run with the attacker while retaining balance and as good a defensive position as possible.

As the attacker pushes the ball a little too far ahead, the

Fig 96   The reverse stick upright tackle.

(a)

(b)

(c)

(d)

(e)

(f)

Stick and Hand Position

During both the preparatory work and the act of tackling, an understanding of the effects of stick and hand position can be extremely useful to the defender.

While the positioning of the stick can be instructive for the attacker, it can be used by the defender as a strategy to influence the movement of the player with the ball. Almost all attackers will move the ball away from the stick and therefore if the defender moves the stick to the left of the ball, the opponent will tend to take the ball the other way. These feints with the stick can also be used to force the attacker to stop their forward movement, lose control of the ball or make a hurried response that may lead to an error.

The most skilful defenders can combine these stick movements with body movements that allow them to take full advantage of the situation. For example, a feint jab tackle in a congested area can force the attacker to push the ball towards the defender's left foot which is a very vulnerable area. If the defender steps backward immediately after the feint and moves the stick to protect the area around his left foot, the ball is often presented to him. When performing these stick feints good balance is vital, so that the body can be moved quickly and easily into the appropriate position. Most of these feints are made using the arms rather than any transference of body weight.

The positioning of the hands on the stick has an important effect upon the tackle. Whenever possible, it is advantageous to have two hands in contact with the stick as it strengthens the tackle. In some instances this is obviously not appropriate, e.g. jab tackle, most reverse stick tackles and some open stick tackles.

The strength of the tackle is related not only to having both hands on the stick but also to the arm strength of the tackler and the use of the body weight in the tackle. The use of the player's body weight depends upon good timing of the tackle and getting it moving forward with the stick. This is not always appropriate and the recognition of how and when to use it will be borne out of experience.

Throughout the preparation and performance of any tackle it is essential that the defender's attention is on the ball, although he may have to be aware of a number of other factors, such as the movement of the stick, body, etc.

The ultimate decision of how and when to make a tackle is borne out of the interaction of all these factors and others, such as previous experience; movement of colleagues and opponents; the position on the field; the tactical situation, etc. These factors combine to influence the ability of the individual and team to regain possession. Their interaction is covered in Chapter 11. Suffice it to say here that the wider the range of experience offered to players during their practice sessions on tackling, the more appropriate their responses in the competitive arena will be.

defender steps toward the ball with the left foot and plays the ball beyond the attacker and into space (Figs 96 (d), (e) and (f)).

There is a wide range of tackles based on these four basic examples, but the general principles illustrated apply to them all. Not all tackles result in clean possession, but the more often players are exposed to the many differing situations, the more likely they are to find successful solutions.

Defending skills are as important a part of the game as attacking skills and they need to be understood and developed in all players. In the game situation they are greatly interrelated and the ability to put them all together is fundamental in the development of strategies for attacking and defending. This will be discussed in the next two chapters.

9

ATTACKING STRATEGIES

Being able to perform all the skills of the game does not guarantee that a player will fit into a team harmoniously. It is the application of these skills and skill patterns that is crucial if a player is to be effective with a team.

Strategies are simply ways of dominating the opposition in given situations. This chapter emphasizes small group situations but it is not difficult to apply both the principles and the examples to larger groups of players.

One of the best methods of developing strategic patterns with players is to formulate the basic principles and then follow a problem-solving approach. The major advantage of this process is that it promotes not merely the search for solutions but also the understanding of the factors that influence any situation. Only understanding provides the players with the opportunity to transfer the knowledge effectively to another situation.

The examples in this and the next chapter will emphasize sharing ideas and concepts developed over a number of years; inevitably, this may exclude a number of valid and creative alternatives. In the actual coaching environment the education of the players would involve the interactive processes which would promote creativity within the players.

It is only possible to work in detail on a few basic strategic patterns but hopefully this will

Fig 97   Richard Leman cuts through the heart of the Pakistan defence, supported by Stephen Batchelor. World Cup, London, 1986. (England won 3-1.)

Fig 98   Imran Sherwani takes on an Australian defender during the 1988 Olympics.

help to identify other situations. The discussion of attacking and defending strategies has a number of objectives:

1.   To emphasize the basic principles that underpin them.
2.   To illustrate a progression for teaching these strategies that can be successfully applied to players of varying age/experience.
3.   To promote a clear framework within any strategy which is understood by all players and allows them to expand upon it.
4.   To encourage players to develop their own strategies and to expand upon those illustrated here.
5.   To give examples of small games/practices that can promote the education of players.
6.   To illustrate some of the questions that can be asked of players to promote understanding.

Basic Principles of Attacking Strategies

The basic principles are very simple and ought to be kept so. The vast majority of successful attacking strategies will incorporate *an incisive or penetrative movement, support ahead, alongside and/or behind the ball* and *a balanced distribution of attacking players appropriate to the situation.*

An incisive or penetrative movement is quite simply getting the ball under control behind a member of the opposition, so that it provides opportunity to expose his defensive situation. The critical word in this simple explanation is 'opportunity', which may manifest itself in a number of ways: to beat the defender who was marking the receiver; to set up a goal-scoring situation; to make an incisive pass to a colleague, etc. However, the factor that allows the group to realize this opportunity is recognition by the players, and this comes from understanding the objectives of the strategy.

Support ahead, alongside and/or behind the ball gives the attacking side a significant advantage when the player with the ball has two or more alternatives (i.e. both width and depth to the attack). The defenders not only have to consider these alternatives but also reposition themselves in the dynamic situation to take account of them. They may find it difficult to provide effectively both marking and covering. It is this process of stretching the defence that helps to tip the scales in favour of the attacking side and again it is essential that the players recognize what is happening so that they can take advantage of the situation.

A balanced distribution of attacking players appropriate to the situation means that the movement of players can create space that can be exploited by colleagues to stretch the opposition defence and penetrate. However, it is important to maximize the effectiveness of this support play. At times it may take too long to provide the ideal level of support to an attacking move and if an opportunity is to be taken it must be attempted even with this slight

118

difficulty (e.g. a rapid counter-attack). In another situation it may be possible to provide extra players in support of the attack but to do so may congest the situation to the point at which the defence gain an advantage.

Clearly, the quality of the support play has a very considerable influence upon the effectiveness of an attacking strategy, and all players in the attacking team should aim to provide support by being available for a pass either directly from the player in possession or via a colleague.

Supporting moves may of course be in a variety of forms where the supporting player may be:

1. Close to the player in possession or some distance away.
2. Stationary or moving.
3. In front of, alongside or behind the player in possession.
4. Moving quickly or slowly.
5. Creating space for himself, or a colleague, or both.

The real skill is to assess which movement will be most beneficial for the particular situation and, in most cases, its success will therefore depend very heavily upon several players moving in harmony.

A vital aspect of support play is an awareness of space. Players must understand how, when and where to move to get into the space most advantageous for their team. This will sometimes require players to move in such a way that creates space for a colleague rather than themselves. Awareness can only be achieved if players use their vision.

In order to achieve successful attacking moves, this understanding of support play must be combined with the skill of the player in possession to give the correct pass in terms of time, speed and direction.

The other major variable influencing support play is, of course, the movement of defenders. Players must be ready to respond to these changes without relinquishing the initiative. Penetration of the opposition's defence is created by putting the ball and a player into a space behind or goalside of a defender. This is achieved by a combination of dribbling, passing and supporting. All these skills along with the concept of making space have been described, but to complete the picture the attackers must be clear in their minds which spaces they are trying to exploit at any one time. There

Fig 99   Jon Potter attacks West Germany in the World Cup semifinal in 1986 (England won 3–2).

is always some space available to the attackers but its size, location and accessibility and the length of time it is available are constantly changing. It is worth assuming as an attacker that good defenders rarely leave large and dangerous spaces behind or goalside of them that are easily accessible. When these spaces do occur the defence will not let the attack exploit them without the latter having to work very hard. The difficulty in scoring goals confirms this.

Coaches should locate the spaces that could be available during any attacking move and assess how they can be exploited, by whom, and what alternative patterns should be used according to the response of the defence. The fact that there is never just one solution to the problem of creating penetrative moves indicates

that players must go through a decision-making process when considering the exploitation of a particular space. Throughout the process, attacking players are reassessing the situation according to the movement of the defenders, and the art of successful team play is the corporate recognition of the best alternative and its execution. These alternatives or patterns of play must be developed so that understanding between players can be refined to the point where team play functions smoothly but not necessarily in a predictable way. Even when the play is predictable, it is performed with such precision that the chances of success are very high.

The raw materials available to a team to develop attacking strategies are the skills of passing, controlling, dribbling,

support play, inter-changing positions and utilizing space. However, it is not sufficient just to have these skills, no matter how abundant they may be in a team. They have to be organized so that the players are able to create attacking strategies (penetrative moves) in a variety of situations. Quality support to create an incisive movement may be needed ahead of, beside, behind, close to or some distance away from the ball.

Principal Coaching Points Related to Quality Support Play

1. The player should not fill the space too early if he thereby attracts a defender, thus negating the advantage.
2. The player should recognize whether he should create the incisive movement, and decide if it is to be by a pass or moving onto or with the ball. He should consider the following questions:
If it is a pass then where is it needed? When? How quickly?
If it is a movement with the ball, then how should the ball be collected?
Is acceleration or deceleration required to take advantage of the situation?
In what direction should the movement be?
If it is a movement onto the ball, how fast should the movement be, and how will the next movement be performed effectively?
3. The player must look for the cues and signals that assist the successful completion of the movement.

Examples of Some Attacking Strategies

The following progressive strategies illustrate some of the

Fig 100 Stephen Batchelor (Great Britain) attacks Karsten Fischer (West Germany) during the 1988 Olympics.

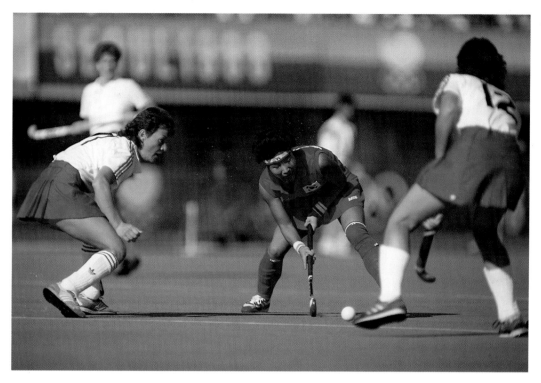

Fig 101   Great Britain defenders close in on the South Korean forward in the 1988 Olympics.

situations that occur in a game situation to aid the understanding and application of the principles related to attacking play. Remember, attackers should start by using large areas, which are then reduced in size to increase the difficulty.

3 vs 1

The three attacking players are challenged to commit the defender to the ball and release the pass to a colleague who can take the ball beyond the defender.

The attackers could be asked the following questions:

Which attacker should commit the defender to the ball?
How is the defender committed?
Where should the support players be?

How is the incisiveness/penetration achieved?
What is the role of the support players?
Where does the receiver wish to receive the ball in order to add the penetrative move?
How fast is the pass made?
What are the effects of one of the flank players committing the defender to the ball?
What has to happen to the distribution of the attackers to increase the chances of success in the last situation?
Can the attackers develop a pattern in which the incisive movement is a pass to a player running forward behind the defender?
What has to happen for this to be successful?
How could a flank player commit the defender in the centre of the area?
How would the support players react?

Questions to the defender that may also help the attackers include the following:

Which person would the defender prefer to bring the ball toward him?
If there is no acceleration in the movement what does it allow the defender to do?
What movements by the attackers cause the defender greatest difficulty?

There are many other questions that can lead to further exploration, identification of key elements, and ultimately, understanding. From this understanding springs the ability to recognize situations in the competitive arena and make them succeed. In reality a 3 vs 1 situation rarely occurs in a game situation but it is useful for developing the basic principles of attacking.

2 vs 1

This situation is more likely to occur in the game and a thorough understanding of the factors that lead to a successful strategy will assist players in 3 vs 2, 2 vs 2 and 1 vs 1.

The following photograph sequences illustrate some of the possible solutions to the 2 vs 1 challenge.

RIGHT TO LEFT PASS
Figs 102 and 104
With support behind/beside ball

Fig 102 (a)   The player with the ball moves forward and to the right. What is the purpose and effect of this movement?
To draw the defender away from the space to be used, enlarging the space available to the support player. To commit the defender to the ball.

Fig 102 (b)   If this were a left flank attack, has the defender taken up an effective position? What are his priorities?
The defender's position is fine because the player with the ball is a greater threat to a run toward goal than his support player.

Fig 102 (c)   When is the pass made?
As the attacker approaches the tackling range of the defender.
In what direction is it made for the support player?
In a direction so that the defender cannot intercept, yet the support player can move onto it.
Could it have been played ahead of the support player?
Yes. But there is greater risk and the position of the defender is more critical.
What else would have to happen for this to be successful?
The pass would have to be made earlier and the support player may have had to move faster.

Fig 102 (d)   Who will provide the incisive/penetrative part of this movement?
The receiver.

Fig 102   A right to left pass with support behind the ball.

(a)

(b)

122

(c)

(d)

123

How could it be achieved?
By accelerating with the ball or giving a return through pass.
Is the situation desperate for the defender if it is a left flank attack?
No. The receiver is still well away from goal and he is goalside.
For what reasons would it have been more dangerous for him if it had taken place in the centre of the field?
The receiver would have had a direct run beyond the defender and toward goal.
How would the defender have positioned himself if it had been in the centre of the field?
More between the players encouraging the player with the ball to keep it; or enticing an early pass to the other player, as it would be a better position to defend. Emphasis on delay to await defensive help.
What might have been the movement of the first player with the ball in this case?

To run straight at the defender to commit him to the ball.

The questions and some of the possible answers in this example show the dialogue that may occur between players and coach. Remember, it is pertinent to ask the defender questions even though the session is orientated to attacking strategies. The answers can provide important information for the attacking players. In the following examples only a few questions are posed. It is now up to the coach and/or player to observe or consider the likely responses and learning points.

With support ahead of the ball
The movement of the passer is similar to before, but notice when the pass is made (Fig 104 (a)). At the same time, earlier or later? Can the passer see the defender while he is

moving with the ball? How does he achieve this? What are the advantages?
Notice the direction of the pass Fig 104 (b). Could the passer have afforded the defender to be more between the two attackers? If this had been the case what could his response have been?
Notice the body position of the receiver. What is his position in relation to the defender? What advantages does this give him? What could be the receiver's next move?
The advantages of both forehand and reverse stick control in this situation should be considered (Fig 104 (c)). If this is a left flank attack, what are the receiver's best alternatives for his next move? Which was the element that contributed most to creating the opportunity to beat the defender: the passer's run, the pass, or the receiver's run?

Fig 103   Jane Sixsmith (England and Great Britain) attacks the Dutch defence at Wembley in 1989.

Fig 104   A right to left pass with support ahead of the ball.

(a)

(b)

(c)

Fig 105   A left to right pass on the reverse stick with support behind the ball.

(a)

(b)

(c)

(d)

Fig 106   Delissen (Netherlands) launches an attack against West Germany at the 1988 Olympics.

LEFT TO RIGHT PASS

Figs 105–108

Reverse stick with support behind the ball

Fig 105 (a)   What are the objectives of the player with the ball?

How is he setting out to achieve them?

Fig 105 (b)   What are the effects upon the defender? What is the position of the support player?

Fig 105 (c)   Can the passer see the receiver?

What restrictions does this put upon the position of the receiver?

What is the passer threatening to do that will influence the thinking and positioning of the defender?

What must the defender do if he wishes to attempt the interception?
How could this help the attacker?
Fig 105 (d)   In what direction is the pass made?
When and how will the penetrative part of this move occur?
Could the pass have been played squarer or even forward with the reverse stick? If so, how?
What alternative did the passer have that sowed doubt in the defender's mind?

Forehand stick with support alongside the ball

Fig 107 (a)   Where is the player in possession running?
What are the objectives of this movement?
Where is the ball positioned?
What are its advantages?
Can the passer see both defender and colleague?
How does this help the passer?
Fig 107 (b)   How has the passer's body position altered?
Is the defender committed to the ball? If so, how far away is the passer?
What is the target for the passer?
How has the receiver's body position altered?
Can the passer still see the receiver and defender?
What advantages does this provide the attacking pair with?
What could be the response of the passer if the defender began to retreat to cause delay?
Fig 107 (c)   Could the pass be played at a variety of speeds?
Does the pass have to be made at a particular moment or is there a longer time frame available to the passer?
If it is the latter, then what alterations to the pass might have to be made?
What else could the passer do other than make the pass?
What might give the player the cue to do this?
How can the incisiveness be added to the movement?

Fig 107   A left to right pass on the forehand stick with support alongside the ball.

(a)

(b)

(c)

Fig 108   A left to right pass on the forehand stick with support ahead of the ball.

(a)

(b)

(c)

(d)

Forehand stick with support ahead of the ball In this sequence (Fig 108) many of the questions relating to the Right to Left Pass on page 122 are relevant and need to be answered. In addition, the following questions should also be considered:

What is the cue for the timing of the pass? Is it the distance between passer and defender or the relative positions of defender and receiver?
Where would the receiver like to be in relation to the defender as the ball arrives? How important is the pace of the pass?
What could the defender do to threaten this move? How could the attackers respond and retain the initiative? What could occur if the defender went closer to the receiver either before the pass is made, or after it is made?

Creating more Space in a 2 vs 1

LEFT TO RIGHT PASS Fig 109
In this situation the defender is close to the receiver, thus inhibiting the movement. The passer could run with the ball but in many instances this could delay the movement so that other defenders reposition themselves and the opportunity for creating more space is lost.

Notice how the receiver can create space by moving slightly forward but more sideways to the right along the line of the potential pass. If the passer can attract some of the attention of the defender then often there is opportunity to make a fast pass close to the feet of the receiver, who is almost level with the defender.

What are the receiver's movements? What are the cues for the pass? What are the reasons for the pass going

Fig 109 Creating more space in 2 vs 1 using a left to right pass.

(a)

(b)

(c)

Fig 110   Creating more space in 2 vs 1 using a right
to left pass.

(a)

(b)

(c)

close to the feet of the receiver?
How will the passer attract the
attention of the defender?
What could happen if the
defender stays close to the
receiver? In what situations
could the receiver collect the
pass on the reverse stick and
turn to the left without
obstructing?

This movement and
variations of it can be used
anywhere on the field. It will
be of benefit to you to go over
the key points related to
Creating the Opportunity to
Receive the Pass in Chapter 5
again.

RIGHT TO LEFT PASS Fig 110
In this instance (Fig 110 (a)) the
receiver has brought the
marking defender infield
deliberately. What advantages
does this create?

The movement is then out to
the left and slightly forward
(Fig 110 (b)). How is this
performed? What is the body
position? How do the feet
move? Where is the receiver's
focus of attention?

Note the cue for the pass (Fig
110 (c)). What must the passer
be doing while the movement
is taking place? Where is the
ball passed? What has the
receiver the opportunity to do?
What could happen if the
defender stayed with the
receiver before the pass was
made?

LEFT TO RIGHT LOOP Fig 111
Fig 111 (a)   What are the
objectives of the passer when
moving from right to left? Is
the angle of the run shallow or
steep? What are the effects on
the defender? What is the
defender concerned about?
Fig 111 (b)   What is the cue for
the pass? Is it the position of
the receiver? Is it the position/
movement of the defender?
Who decides when to pass?
What are the responsibilities of
the receiver?

Fig 111 Creating more space in 2 vs 1 using a left to right loop.

(a)

(b)

(c)

Fig 111 (c) Where is the pass directed? What speed would the pass be? When is the penetrative part of the movement made? What else could the passer do and what would be the cue to this? What are the advantages of this move on the left flank? Could it be used elsewhere?

This section has been done in considerable detail for a number of reasons:

1. The basic patterns and principles in 2 vs 1 can be utilized in 3 vs 2, 2 vs 2 and 1 vs 1 situations.
2. The questioning demands that the challenges be worked through based upon the basic principles outlined beforehand. This will accelerate understanding.
3. The transference of knowledge to other situations will be more likely and powerful if the reader utilizes his own understanding.

3 vs 2

This small-sided game can increase the pressure upon the attacking players as the defending pair are able to combine marking and covering in the confined area, making incisive movements more difficult. The size of the area used will depend upon the experience and ability of the players, but to promote the quality of the interaction it ought to be a rectangle that gives more depth than width to the attacking movement.

The game can be utilized in a variety of areas of the field so that groups of players can develop and refine strategies specific to that zone. It is also advantageous for all players to experience all situations if possible.

The strategic patterns that can be developed in 3 vs 2 are primarily a combination of the

131

principles and options put forward under 3 vs 1 and 2 vs 1. Some of the options are less feasible in particular zones of the field, while others will offer some new variations that can result in incisive movements.

There are a number of very simple factors that the attacking players need to consider:

1.   The commitment of a defender to the ball can create the opportunity for the attackers to change 3 vs 2 to 2 vs 1.
2.   The central player has a key role if the three attackers are moving forward together to isolate or omit one defender, so that the other can be attacked 2 vs 1. This opportunity will not be available for long, so the movement must be as clinical as possible.
3.   Understanding the objectives of the two defenders can help the attackers e.g. where they prefer the ball to be, and what movements of players causes them greatest difficulty.
4.   Can one of the players cause the defence difficulties by leading the attack? What modifications must be made on this to make the game realistic (e.g. an offside line or a time limit on the move)?

These games can be invaluable exercises for promoting the understanding of the factors that have to harmonize to create incisive/penetrative strategies provided that:

1.   The strategies are kept relatively simple.
2.   The dialogue between players as well as players and coach is honest, open and positive.
3.   The players share their knowledge and experience.
4.   The aim is to improve the strategies so that the players

are able to make them happen at match tempo and in competitive situations.

2 vs 2

This is very much more the norm in the game situation and the challenge quite simply is to develop strategies to put the defenders at a disadvantage and provide the attackers with opportunity to get the ball under control and goalside of at least one of the defenders.

The strategies, because of the numerical equality, will inevitably make use of a combination of many of the skills and patterns of movement already discussed. To make them successful in this situation will demand high-quality performance in all the areas.

It may be best to analyse three separate strategies to show how principles and examples can be translated into other strategies and/or areas of the pitch.

LEFT TO RIGHT LOOP Fig 112
The basis of this strategy, already introduced in the 2 vs 1 section, is to cause doubt in the mind of the defenders as to who they are marking.

The aim of Player A is to dribble the ball toward D to attract that defender's attention while pulling the marker C across so that both defenders are close to each other. This movement creates the space previously occupied by A and C for B to utilize.

If B utilizes a shallow-angled run and makes this run while the two defenders are considering the most appropriate response, then the pass from A ought to provide B with the opportunity to beat C on the reverse stick side. The pass must be short and dropped into space so that the receiver can accelerate onto the ball.

This move is particularly useful on the left flank to counter a team who continually force the midfield toward the left wing.

What could be the response if the defender C ran only so far with A and then waited for B to collect the ball on the loop? Could this move be used on the right flank? What modifications would have to be made?

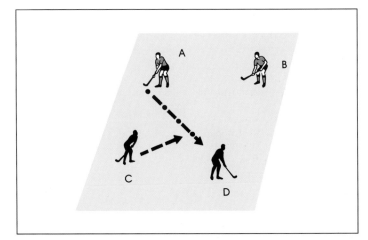

Fig 112   Creating more space in 2 vs 2 using a left to right loop.

132

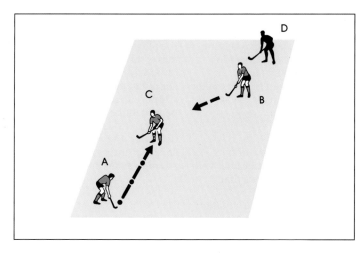

Fig 113   Wall passing in 2 vs 2.

WALL PASSING Fig 113
This is one of the best-known strategies but still requires careful planning to succeed in the 2 vs 2 situation. It is based upon getting one defender ahead of another and exposing the space behind the leading defender and to the side of the other. When executed effectively this changes a 2 vs 2 situation into a 2 vs 1 or even a clear run for one of the attackers.

Attacker A runs toward C with the ball on the forehand stick, looking to commit C to the ball and make a pass onto B's stick. B will aim to play the ball first time into the space behind C for A to run on to.

Attacker B must make certain that he meets the ball nearer to the space than the defender D. If this does not happen the deflection can be intercepted or a tackle can be put in as the ball arrives.

When practising this strategy the following aspects should be remembered by the players:

1.   The initial player (A) in Fig 113 must be able to see all the other three players while moving with the ball.

2.   This player must await the cue from the other attacker before he passes. After the pass, acceleration is essential.
3.   The move can be even more effective if momentum can be built up from the outset. This takes much practice.
4.   The leading attacker waits a few metres to the right of the space in which the deflection will be made.
5.   The timing of the move into this space will depend upon the speed of the movement but at the point of contact the player deflecting must be nearer the line of the pass than the defender.

What could be the variations on this strategy if either defender C steps left to block the pass, or defender D keeps level with or even to the left of the attacker B?

This is an excellent move for the left wing and inside left to exploit the space behind the right half. Where else could it be used?

Could the wall pass be played to a third attacker? In what situations could this be possible? Could the wall pass be used in a 2 vs 2 situation on the right flank? What modifications would have to be made?

DROPPING AWAY FROM A DEFENDER Fig 114
This strategy utilizes two principles: firstly, that the focus of attention of a defender can be split if the receiver makes it very difficult for the defender to see the passer, the ball and the receiver. This split attention provides the receiver with the opportunity to create space to beat the defender. Secondly, that defenders prefer a pass to go in front of them rather than behind.

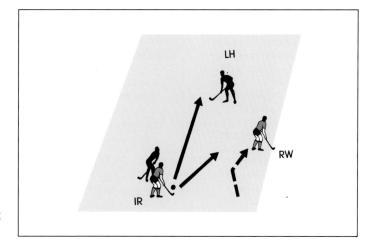

Fig 114   Dropping away from a defender.

133

If in a 2 vs 2 situation (e.g. the inside right and right wing vs the inside left and left half) the inside right has possession and can partly expose the reverse stick side of the inside left, then the left half will move a little infield as there is the threat of a through pass to the right wing or centre forward. The LH will work on the basis that the squarer pass to the RW will provide time for recovering a good defensive position.

Ideally, if the RW cannot receive a pass behind the LH, the next-best position would be as near to level with the LH. This would provide the RW with a very good opportunity to get beyond the LH quickly. If, as the IR advances with the ball, the RW moves forward and infield, the LH will move also because it is the very position that stops the through pass; the LH feels safe.

But, if the RW now steps forward and outward, the LH has a number of problems. The RW cannot easily be watched at the same time as the IR and the ball. To take attention away from one allows the other to make a move.

The options open to the IR depend upon the LH's response to these difficulties. If the LH remains, then a pass can be made to the RW who has dropped away. If the LH moves toward the wing, the channel for the through pass is opened up. If the LH focuses completely on the RW, then the IR can make whatever pass is best, while if the LH focuses completely on the IR, the RW can move into space without the knowledge of the LH. These principles can also be used partly or completely elsewhere on the pitch, e.g. CH and IF; IL and LW; IF and CF; FB and IF.

All these 2 vs 2 strategies need to be supplemented with the detailed information in the sections on passing, receiving, creating space and 2 vs 1 in order to develop a full understanding of how to make them successful.

1 vs 1

Within a game there are endless opportunities for 1 vs 1 but experience shows that, more often than not, interpassing creates a situation in which an attacker has an opponent at a disadvantage. The success of the attacker then depends upon:

1. The player recognizing that the defender is at a disadvantage (e.g. off balance, having to come from a covering position, etc.).
2. The player having the ability to use high-quality stick work and/or changes of direction/speed to beat the defender.

In the less frequent yet equally important situations of the defender not being at a significant disadvantage, then there is an initial decision for the player in possession to make: 'Do I try to beat the opponent?' The decision should be related to the level of support around, the risk, the benefit to the team, etc. If a player decides to take on the defender, then there are some simple principles and strategies that may help.

BASIC PRINCIPLES RELATED TO 1 VS 1
1. The player must use his strengths (e.g. speed, change of direction).
2. He must seek out the weaknesses of his opponent.
3. He must make the defender go backward or change direction rapidly as this often results in loss of balance.
4. He must force the defender to act and then use that to his advantage.
5. He should create doubt with body and stick feints.
6. He should retain balance and control at all times, which will improve his ability to see what the opponent is doing and respond accordingly.

Practising Attacking Strategies

While it is efficient and effective to use small group games and exercises to develop understanding and promote perfection of attacking strategies, there is also the need to put them into a more game-like context. This can be done by playing conditioned games of uneven sides, giving the attackers the opportunity of setting up and succeeding at various strategies (e.g. 7 vs 5 plus goalkeeper).

Other games could be of even sides but in a large enough area to allow the strategies to be attempted.

Only through continual repetition, evaluation and modification will the strategies be honed to the point where they have a very high level of opportunity of success.

The games could emphasize any of the following:

1. Recognizing and attempting 2 vs 1 or 2 vs 2 situations.
2. Setting up a particular attacking strategy, e.g. the 2 vs 2 wall pass or the loop.
3. Attacking strategies in a particular area of the field or between certain players.
4. Counter-attacking utilizing the attacking strategies to set up goal-scoring opportunities.

Fig 115 Great Britain counter-attack against Pakistan in their draw at the Los Angeles Olympics in 1984.

STRATEGIES FOR BEATING PLAYERS 1 VS 1
1. Running with the ball and changing the direction of ball and body.
2. Controlling a pass and flowing into the next movement can create space to expose a defender.
3. Recognizing in a 2 vs 1 when to use the alternative movement to a pass.

All these areas have already been covered. The practising takes time but it is worthwhile not only because of the improvement in the use of 1 vs 1 strategies, but also in the confidence it promotes in the player.

Counter-Attacking

This is a game situation that will certainly require a number of attacking strategies if the team on the offensive is to take advantage of the opportunity.

A counter-attack occurs when a team is robbed of possession in a way that leads to a rapid strike being launched by the team gaining the ball. The attack is fast but does not normally have the ideal support. The defending team, however, are often momentarily caught unbalanced and are therefore susceptible to a fast attack. It is often worth taking the gamble on a counter-attack (or planning for them) as the

135

sudden pressure on the defence can result in considerable dividends.

Principal Coaching Points Related to Successful Counter-Attacks

1. Once possession is gained, the ball must go forward as quickly as possible.

2. This movement of the ball will provide the opportunity to make maximum use of the time and space gained.

3. The point of the counter-attack requires some support as quickly as possible. This may come at the expense of width in the attack.

4. Players should recognize and give this support. Those who cannot give support should not attempt to but rather provide balance to the team.

5. The attacking group must recognize the possible risk of not succeeding and use the appropriate attacking strategies. Practising this aspect of play can only be done at match tempo, otherwise the effectiveness is wasted.

10
DEFENDING STRATEGIES

There is one fact that is astoundingly obvious to all players and coaches. It is not possible to effectively defend the whole 6,000m^2 of the hockey field with only eleven players. While this insight may not be new, it is a valid starting point when considering defending strategies.

The area of pitch which has to be actively considered when defending probably amounts to about 75 per cent. However, 25 per cent of the pitch is protected by the offside rule, so with a clever distribution of players only about half the area will have to be seriously considered. Other areas that can be viewed as low priority are perhaps those that are least likely to be exploited by a direct pass. These are more difficult to assess and will alter dramatically according to the position of the player in possession.

The defending team, though, could have to effectively cover about 50 per cent of the playing area if the opposition had the ball in play at the top of their circle.

Experience points to the fact that only about 35–40 per cent of the field can be defended effectively to give the balance of marking, covering, etc. that all teams seek. This is the simple reason why teams have to have group and team strategies for defending.

One of the principal factors that coaches seem to consider for long periods of time is whether to play person to person or use zonal defence. The most practical answer is that players and teams need to be able to do both, in order to

Fig 116   Australia foils a South Korean attack at the 1988 Seoul Olympics.

Fig 117 A solid tackle. Australia versus South Korea at the Seoul Olympics.

not only the development of a range of skills but also an understanding of how and when to put these into operation, that is recognizing situations and the appropriate solutions.

Regaining possession is achieved by utilizing the core skills of marking, covering, closing down, channelling, tackling and intercepting (controlling). In the competitive situation the importance of each of these skills will vary because the situation is dynamic. It is vital, therefore, not only to be able to perform these skills, but to successfully implement them. This decision-making, both individually and in groups, depends upon an understanding of the fundamental principles of pro-active defence. These principles are drawn up based on the team's defending abilities and a recognition of the primary objectives of the opponents when they have possession.

cope with the wide range of situations within matches. What defending is really about is limiting the opposition's opportunities when they have the ball, so that possession can be safely regained as soon as it is feasible.

Regaining Possession

It is very seldom that the opposition continually present the ball to the defenders without too much work, allowing balance of possession during the game to be about 75–25 per cent. On the contrary, teams have to work both cleverly and with considerable effort to regain possession. The crucial point that many players and coaches fail to emphasize enough is

that defending is a group activity.

When performed in harmony, quality defending influences how the opposition play, reduces their scoring opportunities and increases the chances of the defending team regaining possession. This is not having a defensive approach; rather it is a recognition of what actually happens in matches and being pro-active towards tipping the scales in one's favour.

How well one's team plays while the opposition are in the ascendancy usually has a significant influence upon the result of a match between sides of similar standing – an aspect usually recognized by players and coaches only retrospectively.

The art of coaching players to regain possession involves

Principal Factors Related to Regaining Possession

If the key objective is to regain possession then all the strategies need to be orientated towards increasing the pressure upon the opponents so that they are forced into errors that cede possession. To appreciate the kind of strategies that can be utilized, it is advantageous to understand what the attacking team would like to be able to achieve when they have the ball. These include:

1. Making an incisive forward pass.
2. Creating space to allow an incisive move.
3. Moving forward with the ball.

Fig 118   Warren Birmingham beats Richard Leman in the Great Britain versus Australia Olympic semifinal in 1988.

4.   Making the defenders move around a great deal by retaining possession.
5.   Beating the opponent.
6.   Having time to look for passes.
7.   Creating goal-scoring opportunities.

If these are important priorities to the attacking side, then it is wise that the defenders recognize them when formulating their own. The priorities that are highly ranked by defenders include the following:

1.   Restricting the availability of passes, particularly incisive passes.
2.   Denying forward movement with the ball.
3.   Forcing ball/attackers to less dangerous areas.
4.   Denying space and time.

5.   Forcing the player in possession to attend to the ball rather than look for passes.
6.   Protecting weaker areas in the defensive situation.
7.   Delaying any attack to provide time to organize the defence.
8.   Regaining possession as far up the field as possible.
9.   Not giving easy opportunities to the attacking team.

The relative importance of these priorities will vary both between and during situations. It is impossible to produce a list in order of priority that will hold good for every situation. All defenders must assess the current situation and act in unison with colleagues. This harmony depends upon the quality of the understanding between players, which is

borne out of knowing that decisions made are based upon the same criteria. A fundamental in all group defending is that everyone knows, understands and agrees to the criteria upon which the individual and group decision-making will be based.

Defending Principles that Influence Decision-Making

These criteria or principles are grouped under three headings to provide a foundation on which individuals and the team can build their defensive teamwork. They are: the individual with the ball; the position of the ball on the pitch; and the phase of play.

139

Inevitably, some of the principles fit in two or more categories and there are exceptions to the rule.

The Individual with the Ball

In order to defend the player in possession, the defender should:

1. Stop any incisive passes.
2. Delay or stop forward movement; push backward or sideways.
3. Limit passing opportunities.
4. Force attention onto the ball.
5. Direct toward other defenders or less dangerous areas.
6. Delay tackling until cover is available or chances of success are high.
7. Time his movements so that support defenders can achieve positions that may lead

---

Developing Defending Strategies

This can be achieved in a simple progressive way:

1. The individual skills of defending need to be promoted and developed.
2. Consideration should be given to how small game-related groups (e.g. forwards; full backs; full back, wing half and centre half; wing half, inside forward, wing) need to interact defensively. Practices should then be developed that progress from: a small area to a larger area; numerical equality to inequality in favour of the attacking side; or the small groups to larger groups (e.g. full backs, half backs, goalkeeper).
3. In the larger group/team situation similar progressions to those for the smaller groups should be used. When working on the team orientation/positioning it is advantageous to start from set piece situations and then move onto open play challenges.

---

to subsequent interceptions/tackles.

8. Communicate with defenders ahead of him.

The Position of the Ball on the Pitch

1. If possession is lost on the flank, the defender should

keep the ball there as his colleagues are orientated to that area, resulting in the minimum adjustments to be made.

2. Possession in the centre of the field offers the greatest range of passes. The defender should therefore force the ball wide.

Fig 119   Pakistan defend against Spain during the 1988 Olympics.

3. The defender should restrict fast cross-field switches of the ball, particularly in the midfield, as this stretches the defence dangerously.

4. Possession on the flank allows the defenders on the opposite wing to move further infield, increasing the potential effectiveness of the defence.

5. If the opposition are pressured in their own 25, it is to the defence's advantage if the ball goes to a wing half. This will allow the midfield to provide effective marking and covering while protecting most of the potential long passes out of the defence.

6. When the area of the pitch the opposition can use effectively is small (e.g. along a wing channel) and there are sufficient defenders, then marking ahead of players may be appropriate or even necessary.

7. A congested or small area is easier to defend than an uncongested or large area.

The Phase of Play

1. The team can use restarts to re-establish its defensive pattern or impose pressure on the opponents. If the players always line up effectively at restarts they can begin to dictate how the opposition should play.

2. At some restarts the team could be regrouped further back from the opponents. This would allow the opponents to have the ball, while a strong defensive unit between the defenders' 25 and about 10m into their opponents' half of the field could be retained. When would this be a useful strategy?

3. A sudden counter-attack may require the defenders to retreat and channel rather than tackle until such time as they can regain possession. It may be safer to allow the opponents into the 25 than challenge rashly beforehand. If this happened, where would you try and direct the ball?

Although these defending principles are not always appropriate, they provide the kind of framework that gives the players the opportunity to cope with almost any situation. They will move in harmony because they understand and agree the objectives almost without constant communication. This allows the communication channel to be used for any information pertinent to the situation.

Defending Strategies Application

It is a good idea to return to the examples of attacking strategies (2 vs 1, 3 vs 2, 2 vs 2) and consider what defending strategies can be employed to delay or even counter the movements in various areas of the field. Interestingly, this process will almost certainly produce more valuable knowledge to further develop the attacking strategies. Here are some questions that could be asked to draw out the relevant information:

What is the danger? Where is the threat?
What are the options available to the attacker?
What would the attackers like the defenders to do?
What are the cues that will help the defenders recognize the movements?
Where would the defender(s) prefer the ball to be?
Can the defenders position themselves to achieve this?
Can the player with the ball be isolated from the support?
How else can the move be delayed?
How much delay is needed?
When can pressure be put on the attackers?
What pressure could this be?
Can the pass be enticed and intercepted?
What information do the other defenders need?

The answers to these questions will provide the information to consider in the light of the defending principles outlined. The appropriate strategies will be based on the reservoir of defending skills aided by feedback from previous experience. This process has to take place on the training ground where the situations can be experienced and evaluated many times and the strategies modified and rehearsed. It is also vital that the various positional groupings recognize how the responses may differ according to the position on the field.

The best learning environment for defending strategies is to experience it. The role of the coach is to help ask the searching questions and guide or facilitate the appropriate solutions.

These strategies need to be practised by the whole team for three reasons:

1. To allow the team to recognize the knock-on effect on the defence of, for example, a successful 2 vs 1 down the right wing.
2. To promote solutions to these challenges when they occur.
3. To develop greater understanding and harmony in team defending.

Examples of Some Defending Strategies Figs 120–124

The following five examples demand that the most appropriate strategies be implemented by the team and therefore the individual players' responses be worked out.

SITUATION 1 Fig 120
The right wing has been dispossessed by the left half who is moving forward with the ball. What options are open to the left half? What defending principles apply in the situation? What are the possible responses of the right half, inside right, right back, centre half, centre forward and right wing? Which is the best solution? Are these responses simultaneous or sequential? What are the cues for each player?

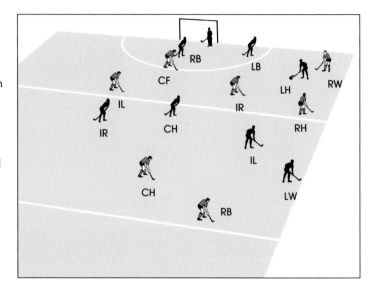

Fig 120   Situation 1.

SITUATION 2 Fig 121
The inside left has intercepted a pass from the right back toward the inside right. What are the likely responses of the inside left and the other attackers? How can these be threatened or even countered by the defence?

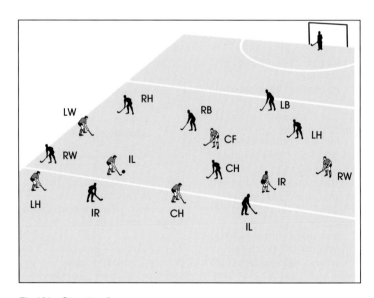

Fig 121   Situation 2.

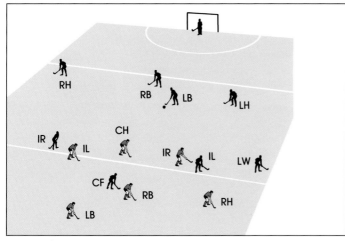

Fig 122   Situation 3.

SITUATION 3 Fig 122
The left back has a free hit. Where should the strikers be positioned? Which defending principles are of highest priority here? How should the strikers and midfield react to a pass to the right half or left half, or a pass to the right back?

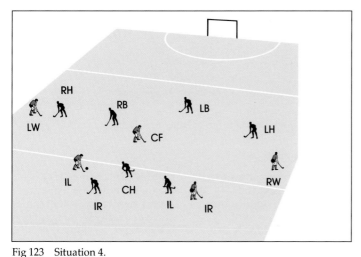

Fig 123   Situation 4.

SITUATION 4 Fig 123
The inside left has beaten the opposing inside right and counter-attacked rapidly. Which defending principles apply? What are the inside left's objectives/options? What are the responses of the defenders to these?

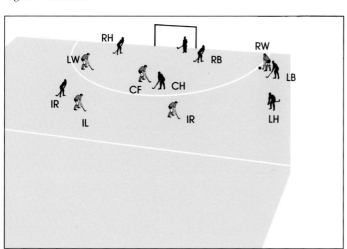

Fig 124   Situation 5.

SITUATION 5 Fig 124
The right wing has beaten the left half and left back in rapid succession. What are the attacking options? Where are the danger areas for the defence? What are the defending priorities? What are the responses of the defenders?

Fig 125   Warren Birmingham (Australia) fails to stop an Alesandro Siri of Argentina during the 1988 Seoul Olympics.

There is one phase of this strategic development that is not analysed here: the point of change from attack to defence and vice versa. The faster an individual, group or team can make the physical and psychological modifications required at this point of change, the more likely they are able to take advantage or regain the initiative. This aspect also warrants training and can readily be integrated into practice sessions.

11
SET PLAY STRATEGIES

Set plays such as free hits, corners and penalty corners take place frequently in hockey, and while the strategies employed in both attack and defence need not be complicated, it is essential that all players involved understand what is happening.

Penalty Corners

These set plays are extremely important and contribute significantly to the outcome of matches. It is not surprising, therefore, that players and coaches spend considerable time on the strategies related to penalty corners.

A mandatory experiment imposed by FIH as from September 1992 demands that the ball be stopped *outside* the circle before any shot is made. While this experiment is in force, the strategies at penalty corners will require some modification although the basic principles and patterns remain sound.

The strategies employed are influenced by a number of the rules of the game and the principal factors are:

1.   The ball must be stopped dead before a shot at goal is made.
2.   The first hit at goal must be hitting the 18in backboards.
3.   The goalkeeper cannot lie down until the first shot is made.
4.   The offside rule only applying to the attacking 25

has made attacking teams at penalty corners more aware of the dangers of a counter-attack.

In Attack

The objectives at penalty corners in attack are quite straightforward:
1.   To make an effective strike on goal.
2.   To make the defence of the penalty corner as difficult as possible.
3.   To recognize the objectives, problems and weaknesses of the defenders and to dominate the situation as much as possible.

In order to perform this group skill, a range of individual skills are required, including injecting the ball, reverse stick control, striking and rebounding.

INJECTING THE BALL
The person hitting or pushing the ball to the stick stopper must be able to do this accurately, smoothly and at the correct speed. This should also be done without giving the defence advance notice of where and when the ball is going.

REVERSE STICK CONTROL
Trapping the ball for the striker should be done with only one touch, if possible, and at the point in the circle that the striker requires it.

The skill is performed with the left hand below the right, the left fingers pointing

downwards and the palm behind the stick facing the ball. The ball is controlled by the left arm 'giving' a little on impact. The stick is horizontal at this point and the ball is controlled near the position of the left hand. It is important that the stopper retains good balance so that there is no obstruction to the striker and variations can be played if necessary. The body position at contact will be stooped, legs bent and arms sufficiently away from the feet to give the striker a clear path.

STRIKING
The hard hit at goal is still a very effective weapon but the best penalty corner routines also employ the flick.

The strike at goal from a penalty corner is more than just another hit or flick, because the pressure of the situation is very different; the expectation to achieve success is high and the margin for error is small. The best strikers maintain good form within this pressured environment and one of the best ways of achieving this is to concentrate upon relaxation prior to the action and the rhythm of the action itself. If the striker is going to employ the flick, then there needs to be a decision as to how the goalkeeper can be deceived into anticipating a hit. This will necessitate consideration of the following aspects:

1.   How late the striker can change from hit to flick.

2. What this change requires in terms of movement, hand positions, etc.
3. Whether this deceives the goalkeeper.
4. What the goalkeeper's response will be if it is not successful.
5. What alternative the striker could use, e.g. flick low.

If the deception is not working, then a variation using a third person may be required.

When using a hit at goal after the ball has been moved within the circle, remember that it is easier to strike a moving ball that comes from the right-hand side, the body being able to be turned into the hitting position before the ball arrives.

REBOUNDING

Many shots at penalty corners result in a rebound opportunity for attackers. Most rebound shots are flicks or slap hits. The situation may require the ball to be controlled before the shot is made or taken away from the goalkeeper or another defender. Players performing this role need to be eager to score yet calm and controlled in their actions.

VERSATILITY

It may not be possible or advisable to have only specialist performers in every position in an attacking penalty corner. Injectors and stick stoppers may also have to

Fig 126   Paul Barber, Great Britain penalty corner striker.

Fig 127　India strike a penalty corner against the USSR.

perform the rebound role. It is important, therefore, that there is versatility amongst the team members to cover all the skills that may be demanded in the attacking penalty corner situations.

Strategies

Generally speaking, most goals that come either directly or indirectly from penalty corners are scored from within an 8m wide channel from goal to the edge of the circle. While this is not surprising, it is important when formulating strategies so as to maximize the opportunity to succeed. Of course, this crucial area of the circle has not gone unnoticed by the defence! However, with only a goalkeeper and four defenders, it is a very demanding challenge for the defence to effectively

cover the whole danger area.

Specific strategies can also be used to expose recognized weaknesses and particular strategies in the defensive unit, like the following:

1.　The goalkeeper may always stand up, thus exposing the corners of the goal.
2.　The defenders close to the goalkeeper may not give good protection and support on rebounds.
3.　The defence may send three people to the top of the circle very quickly.
4.　The leading defender may be easily beaten because he runs out in a certain way.

When establishing strategies, the strengths of the penalty corner team should be assessed and played to using variations on the theme

judiciously. Simplicity is a great advantage as it tends to stand up under the competitive pressure. Complicated moves have a high chance of breakdown.

The examples that follow are not a comprehensive list and some of the variations shown in one can be used in many of them.

Injecting from the Right Wing

The potential disadvantages of injecting from the right wing are that the defence can constantly see the ball and the stick stopper may obscure the striker's view of the ball for a while during the controlling phase.

The advantage to the striker is that he can watch the ball coming toward him, rather than across him, throughout the preparation to strike.

147

SINGLE STICK STOPPER AND STRIKER Figs 128 and 129
In Fig 128 the following attacking moves are made:

1. Direct strike at goal with either a hit or flick.
2. The stick stopper pulls the ball to the right with the reverse stick and shoots. Could the striker help with a dummy hit?
3. As in (2), but the ball is slipped back to the striker. When would this be used?
4. The striker slips the ball forward for a hit or flick at goal. When could this be used? What are the problems concerning the deception of the defence?

The players in Fig 129 approach the defence with these moves:

1. The striker hits the ball outside the right post for the injector to deflect into goal. This can be very effective but there is a risk in striking the ball hard but not at goal.
2. The ball is played to the support player on the right

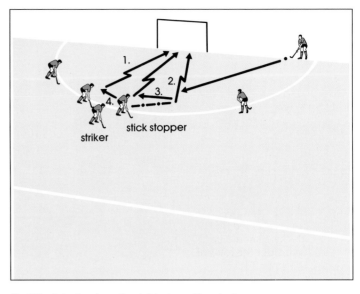

Fig 128   Injecting from the right wing with a single stick stopper and striker.

who puts it back into the space behind the leading defender. Who could play the first pass and how? What deception could be put into the move and by whom? When would it be most effective?
3. The striker plays the ball between the defender and

goalkeeper to the attacker coming in from the left wing position. How could the defender be enticed to leave this gap?
4. The ball is slipped to the first support player on the left who moves it on to the left wing support. What are the responsibilities of the first support player?

DOUBLE STICK STOPPER AND STRIKER Fig 130
When using two sets of stick stoppers and strikers, it is advantageous to have at least 3–4m between them so as to maximize the deception without going so wide that the angle of shot is poor. The aim is to make the defence doubt and perhaps even badly position themselves if they fail to read the situation effectively.

If the deception is going to be effective, then it is wise to keep the strikers in the same positions during the variations.

These options exclude the direct strike (hit or flick), which have already been covered.

Fig 129   Single stick stopper and striker from the right wing.

1. After the stick stop the striker dummies a hit at goal. The ball is then played by the stick stopper (reverse stick) to the right where it is stick stopped again (open stick) for the second striker to hit. What is likely to have happened to the defenders if the dummy strike is good?

2. After the stick stop, the ball is passed left to the other striker to make a first-time hit. When would this be effective? What are the difficulties of this move for the attacking side?

3. If the team decided that only six attackers should be involved, consider the roles of the stick stopper and striker when they are not involved in a move.

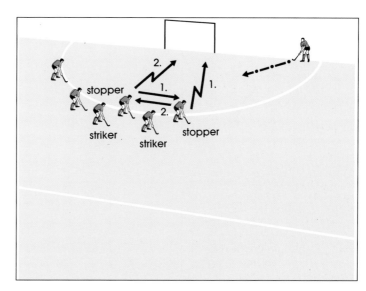

Fig 130   Double stick stopper and striker.

Fig 131   The Canadian penalty corner defence take evasive action at the 1984 Olympic games in Los Angeles.

149

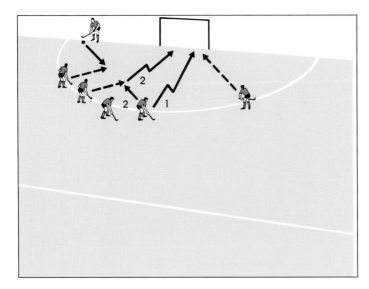

Fig 132   Injecting from the left wing with a single stick stopper and striker.

Injecting from the Left Wing

SINGLE STICK STOPPER AND STRIKER Fig 132
1.   Direct strike at goal with either a hit or a flick.
2.   After the stick stop, the striker dummies the hit and the stick stopper slips the ball forward to the support player to flick or hit. What would be the movement and positioning of this player?
3.   Are there other alternatives using this basic format of players?

DOUBLE STICK STOPPER AND STRIKER Fig 133
1.   One of the two strikers makes a direct strike. If the line of the pass to the strikers can be as similar as possible, then the deception is greater. The first stopper can move in and allow the ball aimed for the second pair (B) to pass close by the right-hand side of the body while taking up the stopping position.
2.   The injector passes to pair B. The strike is dummied and the ball is played forward to the striker of pair A to shoot. The stopper of pair A has moved on an arc to become a rebounder.
3.   The same move as in (2), but it is performed by pair A and the pass goes to the support player. What would be the role of pair B in this move?

4.   If the defence send two people out to counter the double stick stop, what strategy could be employed?
5.   How could the roles be deployed if only six attackers were to be used?

In Defence

The principal objectives when defending penalty corners are:

1.   To minimize the effectiveness of any attacking strategy.
2.   To protect the relevant danger areas.
3.   To clear the ball from the circle quickly and safely.
4.   To recognize the likely attacking strategies.
5.   To dominate the situation.

There are a number of specialist roles within the defensive penalty corner team. However, all members need to have high-quality defending skills, be calm and decisive under pressure and be alert to recognize danger points as they arise.

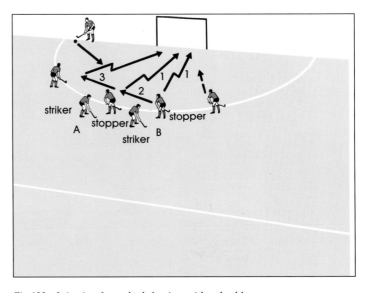

Fig 133   Injecting from the left wing with a double stick stopper and striker.

150

THE ROLES Fig 134

For the purposes of explaining the most common roles assigned to players within the penalty corner routine, players will be distributed as shown in Fig 134.

The goalkeeper (A) This player clearly has a very specialized role at penalty corners. In modern hockey on artificial turf pitches most goalkeepers are using the lying or dropping technique in accordance with the rules. This should be done only with the proper equipment and after correct coaching. At the penalty corner goalkeepers may come out about 3–5m and wait to see what the attackers do or even charge much further and slide pads leading at the ball.

Whatever particular strategy the goalkeeper uses will influence the roles of the other defenders. In this case the goalkeeper is staying back and dropping on his right side to cover all but about 0.6m of the goal. Some goalkeepers prefer to cover up to the post on their feet side and use their stick and left hand to protect as much of the goal as possible on the other side with a defender behind them at that side as security. While there are some advantages to this means of covering up, it requires very skilful use of the hands and can be more difficult for the person on the post.

Goalkeepers who stay back, look for cues as to the intentions of the striker and react accordingly. This again is a very skilful process and goalkeepers can be helped by other defenders recognizing particular characteristics of certain strikers. If defenders are able to recognize cues and know what is going to happen, it gives them an important psychological advantage over the attack.

Fig 134   The most common roles of players during the penalty corner.

The leading defender (B)
This player has to be quick enough to put some pressure on the striker, but such is the quality of the routines and the playing surface at the highest level that very few penalty corners are charged down by this player. In order to get the very best start from the line (usually to the left of the goalkeeper so that the latter's vision is not obscured) this player must recognize what the injector does immediately prior to pushing/hitting the ball. What part of the body is the cue?

Another role of B is to inhibit any variations in the corner routine that could result in a significant opportunity for the attackers. For example, if the ball is passed to the attackers' right, it is important that the leading defender does not allow a return pass to the top centre of the circle. It is better for the defence for the shot to come from the inside right position than the ball be returned to the striker in the centre, because the rest of the defence, especially the

goalkeeper, will have reorientated to the new position.

This secondary role demands that B is in balance as the top of the circle is approached. To charge the strike down is therefore an unreasonable expectation.
Defender C This player has a very varied role. If there is a direct shot at goal he must be ready to help clear away any rebound from the goalkeeper because the opposing centre forward and probably another forward will be very close.

Another aspect to the role is to recognize corner variations:

1. Where the striker makes a slip forward and left to another attacker to shoot, defender C must pressure the shot even though it is difficult to stop it. The only way this shot can be countered is by moving to a much higher position in the circle earlier.
2. A pass on the goalside of C to an attacker coming in from a left wing position can be very effective and it must be guarded against.

151

3. If the ball is moved to the inside right position C should look to protect the area around the penalty flick spot, which is a danger area.

Player D This role also has a number of responsibilities. The principal one is to assist the goalkeeper by clearing rebounds from the pads and body on the forehand stick. This is a particularly important role when the goalkeeper has gone down into the lying position from which it is much more difficult to make clearances. It is important therefore that this player be quite close to the goalkeeper when he makes a save; otherwise any rebound falling in the area in front of the goalkeeper is likely to be gathered by a forward before any defensive support can get there.

A second aspect to this role is to recognize corner variations and the consequent danger points:

1. A pass to the attacking inside right position will demand that this defender closes down the shot as quickly as possible. Staying in the position to the left of the goalkeeper will not be very useful as the goalkeeper will want to move there. The shot will probably take time to set up if the receiver has to control the ball, so there is time to move forward.

2. Passes to the attacking left will demand that this player moves in that direction to protect the danger area between goalkeeper and penalty flick spot.

Player E The defender on the line has to be able to stop or deflect to safety shots up to 0.5m above the ground. This position demands considerable coolness and concentration under pressure. A second aspect to the role is to be aware of the flicked shot above the dropping goalkeeper which will probably necessitate a repositioning within the goal

to make a save a little easier.

The final aspect of this player's duties is to recognize the variations to the corners and move accordingly. If the goalkeeper moves during a variation so that the player is unable to see the ball, then it is likely that there is a better position for either the defender or the goalkeeper. This will necessitate an evaluation of the danger points and the best deployment of the limited resources.

All these roles and their interaction demand considerable practice if this defending unit is going to achieve the stated objectives. When a team is practising penalty corners, it is important to remember that both the attacking and defending strategies need to be done initially without too much competition. It is also advisable not to attempt to practise both attack and defence simultaneously; they need

Fig 135   India's penalty corner players keep their eyes on the ball. Seoul Olympics, 1988.

each other's help but the emphasis ought to be on one aspect only. A competition of a rapid succession of five corners, properly umpired, is good for concentrating the players' minds and intensifying pressure similar to match conditions, but it needs to be used judiciously.

Now that the basic defending roles at the penalty corner have been outlined, it is a good idea to consider how one's defensive unit would respond to the attacking strategies described previously, and take the ideas to the training ground – the environment where the most important modifications are usually made. Rule changes demand detailed attention to roles.

Corners Figs 136–138

Most teams look to put sufficient pressure on the defence in their own circle to translate a corner into either a shot at goal or a penalty corner.

The two principal strategies aimed at achieving these objectives are either a very hard hit into the congested area or a pass to a player who uses individual skill to create the opportunity. Many corners are played into one of the two shaded areas in Fig 136 either directly from the corner or after a short pass to a colleague to improve the angle for the pass. The latter move is often a very short pass from the wing followed by a loop around the back of the support player to receive a return pass about 5–7m from the goal-line. The area nearest the goal-line can, if penetrated, create a goal-scoring opportunity from a deflected shot (centre forward or left wing), or a difficult situation for a defender trying to control the ball, which could lead to a shot or a penalty corner.

The shaded area on the edge of the circle can be used by attacking players to control the ball on the forehand stick and pressure a defender or pass toward the goal for the centre forward. The inside right can move toward the goal on the goalside of the defender and then step out to receive the pass. The centre half can use a similar move or, if the inside right stays within the circle, a movement towards the ball. How does this move need to be performed (bearing in mind body movements, timing, cues, position and speed of pass)?

Defensively the line-up can be as in Fig 136, where the left wing is threatening the passes to the inside right and centre half. The left half and left back are positioned so that they are nearer the ball than other attackers but far enough away to control the ball. Getting too close is rather foolhardy as a player rarely stops anything. The attacker may play the ball short to the right half, but that immediately changes the

Fig 136 Most corners are played into one of the designated areas either directly from the corner or after a shot pass to a colleague to improve the angle for the pass.

Fig 137   The Indian corner defence under starting orders!

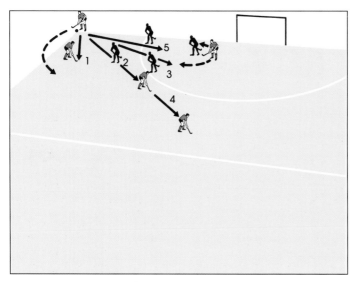

Fig 138   Attacking moves when performing a
corner from the left wing.

situation and the left wing would close him down rapidly.

One possible alternative is for the left half and left back to take up slightly different positions, with both players the same distance from the ball, but now the left back covers the pass close to the baseline while the left half positions himself 2–3m infield from the baseline. The advantages of this formation are that the left half is able to force the hitter to play the ball further away from goal, because the large gap on the left half's reverse stick is covered by the left back's forehand stick and the left back's reverse stick is covered by the goalkeeper.

Corners from the Left Wing

Similar defensive patterns to those in Fig 138 can be established for corners from the left wing, including the following attacking moves:

1. The left wing passes to a support player who dribbles as if to go round the forehand stick of the defender, but who plays the ball back to the left wing who has looped behind his colleague.
2. The inside left, or player who best finds space when marked tightly, manipulates the opponent and receives a hard pass onto his open stick. The skill is to let the ball come right across the body in order to exploit the defender's reverse stick side.
3. The inside left deliberately pulls the defender toward the edge of the circle and a similar pass to that in (2) is played to the centre forward as he moves towards the ball.
4. As in (3), but the inside left keeps the defender inside the circle and the ball goes to the centre half.
5. If the right half is weak, or the gap is there, then a pass to the centre forward is very dangerous for the defence.

Free Hits

Except when the free hit is within 5yd of the attacking circle, players from the side given possession can be within 5yd of the ball. This alteration to the rule has made the vast majority of restarts much more straightforward. There are many simple and effective moves at free hits and restarts to get the ball to a player who is marked (*see* page 81). The following are broad principles that can apply to most free hit/restart situations.

In Attack

1. Penetrative passes from free hits demand high-quality timing from both passer and receiver. The opportunity is only there for a short time and both parties must seek to exploit it by working for each other.
2. Take the free hit as quickly as the situation demands. Many free hits are spoilt by a rash decision.
3. In a player to player marking situation a defender may be deliberately enticed away from an area that is to be used by the same attacker or a colleague. The timing of the movements of the receiver and the pass is crucial, so that sufficient space is created to make the next move.
4. When zonal marking is employed, the defenders are less concerned with following the players and more orientated to cover the spaces into which the ball is likely to go with the intention of intercepting it. The ability to pass accurately and with deception to beat the potential interceptors plus the intelligent movements of the receivers is essential.
5. Short free hits quickly taken can maintain the momentum of the attack, thereby retaining the pressure on the defence as they do not get time to reorganize during the period when play has stopped. In these situations it is important that the strategy results in the play moving forward, the player in possession being able to see the game ahead and have a choice of passes.
6. The person who is supporting the player on the ball at the free hit should assess the situation before the short pass is made so that the most appropriate strategy for the team is implemented. For

example, a long cross-field pass rather than short interpassing may be needed.
7. Other support players should also provide information to assist the players close to the free hit.
8. Use the opportunity of the free hit/restart to set up attacking strategies, e.g. 2 vs 1, 2 vs 2.
9. The phase of the game and area of the pitch may influence how the free hit/restart is taken.

In Defence

1. Players must constantly concentrate on what is happening, otherwise an opportunity can be presented to the opponents.
2. Communication is essential to assist reorganization as the game continues or restarts.
3. Closing down, channelling, etc. are even more important as defenders have to be further from the ball than the opponents.
4. Any repositioning necessary has to be done immediately the free hit is awarded as the time between the award and the restart is short.

Free Hits Close to the Attacking Circle
Figs 139–140

This area requires a little more analysis because once the free hit is within 5yd of the circle, everyone except the attacker on the ball has to be 5yd away. The likelihood of a quick free hit in this situation is therefore diminished.

Free hits within about 10yd of the goal-line tend to be viewed in the same light as corners. The most common strategy is the hard strike into the circle with the objective of getting a deflected shot or

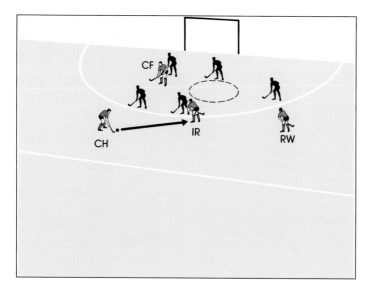

Fig 139   Free hit close to the attacking circle.

putting a defender under considerable pressure. The most profitable line for these passes is toward the far goal post or outside it. This provides opportunity for at least two attackers.

Nearer the top of the circle the hard hit toward goal is less effective because the depth of the attack is less; normally there is only one player able to get to a hard forward pass. This does not negate its use, merely increases the odds against likely success. In these positions other set strategies are normally employed with

the objective of creating a goal-scoring opportunity or a penalty corner. The principal part of the strategy is creating sufficient space in a very congested and tight marking situation to control the ball and create an opportunity for a shot or the winning of a penalty corner.

In the examples in Figs 139 and 140 the following factors should be carefully considered: who starts the move? How can this be signalled? When is the pass made? What type of pass and where to? How can the intention be disguised?

On the forehand side   In Fig 139 the centre half strikes a free hit hard to the forehand stick of the inside right who has previously moved his marker into the circle and then retreated smartly as the hit is made. The inside right initiates the move. The right wing stays wide to hold the left half out. The aim of the inside right is to exploit the reverse side of the marker or project the ball into the shaded area toward which the centre forward will be moving.

What instructions could be given to the marker of the inside right? Could the centre half threaten the pass? If he does, how do the attackers respond? If there was an extra defender back, where should he stand?

From right to left   Fig 140 this time shows the pass from right to left. In the first move the inside left moves into the circle and then retreats to receive a pass on his forehand stick and looks to drive into the circle. The second move is based on the previous one but in this case the inside left stays in the circle and the left wing cuts across for the ball onto his forehand stick. Possible responses to any defensive moves should be considered.

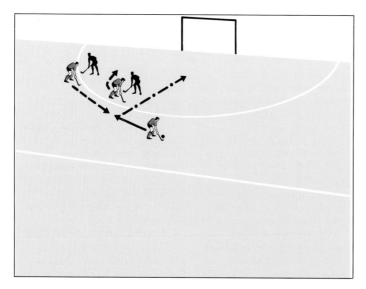

Fig 140   A free hit close to the attacking side from right to left.

Fig 141   Australia line up to defend a penalty corner at the 1986 World Cup in London.

Defending Free Hits

Most teams employ a mixture of player to player and zonal marking but normally there are more defenders than attackers. Every attacker is therefore marked; the more likely the attackers are to receive a pass and the closer they are to goal, the tighter the marking. Recognizing the intentions of the attackers is a very important part of defending. This can help the defender stop the forward creating sufficient space or counter the planned subsequent move. Players should learn to be aware of the body movements of players when they are trying to create space so that they are not so easily deceived by opponents.

Also, if the hit toward goal is an important strategy for the attacking side, the defence should recognize this and block this path as effectively as possible. Experience shows that the defender closest to the ball can line up between the ball and the zone in front of the goal, covering as much of the area as possible with the body and forehand stick. The goalkeeper is the best person to direct the defender. Once this position is set up, the locations of the other defenders can be determined quickly in accordance with their marking and covering responsibilities.

Restarts in the Defending Area

These restarts deserve some attention in the coaching of a team as they occur regularly in the match situation and are potentially the starting point of many attacks.

In most matches the ratio between defenders and strikers is 4:3. Teams play with either a sweeper and three others or two full backs and two wing halves. Whatever the basic pattern and the specific roles allocated to these players, there is normally an extra defender.

In many restarts in the defending area all of the opponents are between the ball and the goal which the team in possession are attacking. Apart from the attacking principles put forward under Free Hits on page 155, there are another two specific to these situations:

1.   The ratio of 4:3 in favour of the team in possession should be utilized. Strategies can be developed to manipulate the opponents so that the attacking team get both the ball and one of the four defenders

157

Developing Strategies at Restarts in the Defending Area Fig 142

There are innumerable strategies a coach can develop in this area of the pitch to get the ball and players moving forward in an attack.

The following challenge is to get the ball and one of the four defenders behind the opposing strikers and into the designated area.

Some of the questions that need to be answered to find a successful strategy include:

Are the opposing forwards marking if a defender moves forward without the ball?

Where should the forwards be positioned so that the strategy can work? How can they be manipulated?

Which defender moves forward? Does the player go with or without the ball? What factors influence this decision?

What can the inside forward/midfield player do to help this strategy?

How can the centre half/midfield be used?

If a defender moves into the space without the ball, how is the ball then delivered, by whom and what are the cues for the passer?

What do the opposing forwards want the defender to do?

How can the other defenders help the strategy succeed?

Are the defenders able to maintain possession and the forward momentum as the situation changes due to decisions made by the opposition?

What do the defenders do if the opposing forwards retreat 15m; or the centre forward stands between the fullbacks; or they invite the pass to the wing half?

New questions will constantly arise as a strategy is developed on the training ground. All of the strategies will have their foundations in the fundamental skills and patterns of play (creating space, passing, 2 vs 1, 3 vs 2, etc.) that have been investigated in previous chapters.

Attempt to identify the movements that create these opportunities so that players can recognize, understand and reproduce them.

Having experimented initially with the right-hand side of the field, transfer the challenge to the left. This is an underused area from which to launch attacks but one that can be very effective.

The next stage, once the ball and defender are in midfield, is to recognize and utilize the extra player advantageously (*see* Attacking Strategies in Chapter 9).

beyond the opponents' line of three strikers.

2.   Many teams utilize the wing halves as points of distribution from these restarts. This is more successful if the wing half is able to move forward with the ball. If this player is stationary, then the balance begins to swing toward the opponents as they can close down and pressure wing halves more effectively than they can central defenders. The simple guideline that often helps players is that passes to wing halves in these situations should allow them to move forward with the ball or should pull the opposing forwards across the field to provide the opportunity for a fast switch of the ball to release another defender to go forward.

Building attacks slowly from the defensive quarter is not always appropriate; if a defender can make a successful pass directly into midfield or further, then that should be done. The strategies explored in this section will increase the repertoire available to a team because in reality not all restarts can be done quickly enough to ensure rapid penetrative moves. Other solutions are also necessary.

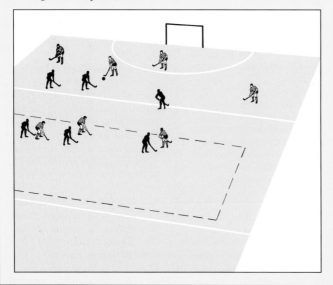

12
ADVANCED GOALKEEPING

The revolution in playing standards brought about by the advent of artificial pitches has meant great changes in the art of goalkeeping.

The history of such changes started in the early 1970s when one of Great Britain's many talented goalkeepers, Peter Mills, developed his own technique of 'diving' or 'flopping' to his left at short corners and stopping the often high ball with his hand or body. Modern goalkeepers should note that he wore no chest protector, no mask or helmet and had somewhat flimsy gloves! This was, however, before the introduction of stiffened sticks, and matches were played on grass. The net result was that the ball did not travel as quickly as it does today. Peter dominated the circle; he was a big man able to psychologically overpower forwards and penalty corner strikers. He was ahead of his time in many ways, as the next developments came in about 1978.

Great Britain was still producing outstanding goalkeepers. Ian Taylor had taken over from John Hurst in early 1978 as the first choice England goalkeeper, reproducing the domination over attackers and strikers that Peter Mills, and before him Harry Cahill, had shown. He relied on tremendous reflexes, outstanding agility and sheer talent to perform superbly in both the World and European Cups of that year. In fact, Ian was voted goalkeeper of the tournament in the Hanover European Cup.

Holland were the most

Fig 143   Pakistan's goalkeeper slides out beyond the penalty flick spot to save an England penalty corner shot, and is watched by Norman Hughes and Stephen Batchelor. World Cup, 1986.

Fig 144 Ian Taylor and Paul Barber await a centre during the World Cup semi final against West Germany in 1986.

outstanding in that tournament, beating England 5–0 to cruise into the semifinals, but they were beaten by Germany in the final, partly due to the German goalkeeper lying down about 4–5m from his line to block the striking of the great Paul Litjens. This was a new development which was viewed sceptically by many other goalkeepers present, a view which was upheld two years later when the goalkeeper concerned, Klaus Ludwiczaq, had to have a testicle removed after applying this technique in a match against Australia. He was hit at

a penalty corner by Jim Irvine and subsequently retired from international hockey. This unfortunate occurrence underlines the most important principle: that modern goalkeeping requires total protection.

England toured Australia in 1981 and Taylor enhanced his reputation as the world's finest goalkeeper by goalkeeping superbly to deny Australia victory in an international series at home for the first time. He was able to stand at corners and use 'traditional' goalkeeping techniques to keep the Australians at bay. The last test in Perth on

Astroturf was lost, however, and goalkeepers all over the world were beginning to experience the difficulties of defending penalty corners on artificial surfaces using 'traditional' techniques.

Great Britain had first experienced this in 1979, again in Perth, at the Esanda Tournament. During the next two years the ability of strikers to convert corners increased so that scores of 6–3, 7–4, 7–5, etc. became commonplace.

Contributory factors toward this were stiffened sticks (increasing power), a greater skill level (brought about by playing on artificial surfaces)

and the fact that the nature of the surface meant that the ball could be hit consistently harder (no divots!). The strikers were once again in the ascendancy. The Rules Book attempted to lower the importance of penalty corners by removing the hand stop, but as usual players turned this to their advantage by inventing the horizontal stick stop. Now the ball could be propelled from the goal-line to the stopper even harder, allowing the defence less time to break down the routine.

The next goalkeeping development to counter this first came to light in 1982 at the World Cup in Bombay on grass! (This was the last major tournament to be held on natural grass.) The embryonic Soviet Union side were defending resolutely with their goalkeeper Vladimir Pleshakov lying down in a way reminiscent of Ludwiczaq. England dominated them in their pool match but Paul Barber just could not get the better of Pleshakov and the result was a 2–2 draw. Again, the goalkeepers present expressed reservations about this method, particularly as Pleshakov wore as little padding as Ludwiczaq had done. Also at this tournament, some goalkeepers were charging penalty corners 'indoor style' with a degree of success. There was no doubt that by mixing their defence of corners, goalkeepers were making strikers think a little more and reducing the scoring rate.

The charging goalkeeper was a feature of the 1983 European Cup in Amsterdam. Teams with charging or prone goalkeepers did significantly better than teams with 'standing' goalkeepers. The tournament was on Astroturf, but the goalkeepers were not particularly well protected. The German duo of Ludwiczaq and Schleman were particularly adept at 'charging'. Pleshakov eclipsed Taylor to become Goalkeeper of the Tournament chiefly because he was the master at lying prone, reading 'flick shots', going down and getting up fast, etc. Veryan Pappin achieved success with the charging technique for Scotland as did Simon Rees in a memorable 0–6 defeat of Wales by Germany (it could have been more!). Ian Taylor and John Hurst for England, however, were adamant that this was 'not goalkeeping' and in fact 'down right dangerous'; a fact brought home to all by the head injury inflicted on the excellent French goalkeeper, when struck on the helmet at a penalty corner in the match against Germany. His flimsy helmet disintegrated and he took no further part in the tournament. Thankfully he made a full recovery.

In the final, Pleshakov had a fine game defending corners in the prone position, whilst the Dutch goalkeeper, Pierre Hermans, charged with some success. Neither wore significantly more protection. The score was 3–3 after extra time, the Dutch winning on penalty strokes. In 1984, Ian Taylor was finally persuaded to adopt the techniques of charging and lying, just before the Olympic games began in Los Angeles. He said he would do so if he was provided with adequate protection. The outcome is, of course, well known! Ian, hurling himself from his goal at penalty corners, saved virtually everything thrown at him and re-established himself as the World No. 1.

Since then, the technique has been refined, more of the world's top goalkeepers have adopted the philosophy of protecting themselves adequately and at present, the goalkeepers are once again in the ascendancy over the strikers.

In 1989 the Hockey Rules Board adjusted the rule covering dangerous play by the goalkeeper. This followed a series of serious accidents involving less experienced goalkeepers emulating their more illustrious counterparts and lying down without full protection. The term for this is 'logging' and it is fair to say that many international goalkeepers were going down very early and allowing the ball to hit their prone body. In Britain, top goalkeepers had attempted to go down as late as possible, reacting to the shot. The aim of the rule change has been to promote and further this *reaction to the shot*. The goalkeeper may not go down *before the first shot has been made* and thus logging has been banned.

To conclude, it has become apparent that goalkeeping in modern hockey on artificial surfaces requires the utmost protection and the adoption of techniques which are different from those used on grass. It is most important that grass techniques or standard goalkeeping techniques are learned *before* progression to more advanced techniques suitable for artificial surfaces. Without these fundamental techniques the goalkeeper will not be able to perfect his goalkeeping on artificial surfaces.

Within this chapter there are photographs of many practices for goalkeepers. You will see that most of them have been set up on a grass area utilising tennis fencing as a makeshift goal to illustrate that the ideal facilities, while desirable, are not essential.

Equipment Fig 145

As has already been stated, serious injury has become more likely since the advent of stiffened sticks, artificial surfaces and higher playing standards. Total protection is therefore necessary and the equipment required when performing at the highest level includes the following:

1. An (ice hockey) helmet with visor and throat protector is essential. The throat protector is important protection for the vulnerable throat area.
2. The very least that should be worn on the arms are elbow protectors. Short corner defence using the 'diving' technique should not be attempted *without full arm protection*.
3. A well protected ice hockey abdominal guard worn with a 'slip in box' underneath gives extra protection.
4. Gauntlets with a well-padded left palm, thimble protection for the fingers and padding for the right thumb are ideal. The backs of the hand and wrist areas should also be well padded.
5. Padded short protection is necessary to adequately protect the front of the thighs and the hip area, and to protect against damage from abrasive artificial surfaces.
6. Leg-guards need to be light with foam bolsters to protect the legs. They should be made of top-quality material in order to minimize premature wearing.
7. Like the leg-guards the kickers need to have adequate foam protection, although most kickers need extra foam padding along the instep area.
8. Some goalkeepers like to wear knee-pads and shin-guards under their kit for added protection. It is worth mentioning that no equipment exists which offers 100 per cent protection from injury and the modern goalkeeper needs to keep a good supply of high-density foam available with which to supplement his kit.
9. Finally a stiff, light indoor stick should be used for maximum speed of movement and reverse stick tackling.

Tremendous advances are now being made by the leading hockey manufacturers in the development of lightweight goalkeeping kits using high-density foams. These advances should go some way to restoring the lack of mobility that the wearing of protective equipment causes. It must be emphasized that the basic techniques which the first set of practices aim to develop *must* be mastered before full kit is donned.

Standard Goalkeeping Techniques

These techniques must be learned *without* wearing full artificial surface kit. Light balls or tennis balls are a useful way of practising these techniques.

A position of readiness (Fig 146) which is similar to that used in other sports like tennis must be adopted. Weight should be slightly forward, on the toes. The whole body should be alert but relaxed. The stick should be held in such a way that it can be moved into action quickly.

Remember, the position of the head is important. It should always be looking at the ball and, if possible, be behind the line of the ball. The basic rule *head over knee over ankle* is fundamental (Fig 146).

Practices to Learn and Improve Basic Techniques

Throughout his career the goalkeeper must maintain his

Fig 146 The player's head looks at the ball and is behind the line of the ball.

basic techniques. Just as a golfer or snooker player needs to practise his swing or cue action, so a goalkeeper must practise the basics upon which advanced goalkeeping is built. He can practise with another goalkeeper but the best method is to have regular training sessions with an experienced coach; the

following practices are set up so that the goalkeeper and coach can work together.

PRACTICE 1 Fig 147
The coach hits balls from the top of the 'D' at the goalkeeper who plays them back to the coach under control. The coach looks for correct weight, balance and positioning.

Fig 147 Practice 1.

Fig 148   Practice 2.

PRACTICE 2 Fig 148
The coach hits balls from the top of the 'D' *at* the goalkeeper who has to save clear to the side, or safely out of the circle. The goalkeeper is now combining power with his technique.

PRACTICE 3 Fig 149
The coach now lines up balls about 10m from the goal-line and advances along the line striking the balls at the goalkeeper or down the channel either side of each leg. The coach or feeder must hit *sympathetically*; he is trying to improve the goalkeeper's technique under pressure. Once again weight must be forward and power exerted to clear the ball from danger. As the goalkeeper becomes more confident the balls can be moved nearer to him. (It is vital that the practice does not become an ego trip for the feeder, who can easily score against the world's best goalkeepers from this range if he so desires.)

These three practices are used by the coach to assess whether a particular leg is weak and requires extra work. It has been assumed that the coach has decided that the left leg is weaker and indeed requires extra work.

PRACTICE 4 Fig 150
The coach now uses light balls or tennis balls, even if he did not use them for Practices 1–3, not only to protect himself from injury, but also the goalkeeper.
   The coach kneels 4m from the goal-line (Fig 150 (a)), with a supply of balls, opposite the post corresponding to the goalkeeper's weaker side. The goalkeeper stands in the middle of the goal. The coach feeds the balls underarm just inside the post at heights between knee and floor and the goalkeeper has to dive across to that side to save clear (Fig 150 (b)).
   His momentum should take him through the action and back to the position of readiness for the next shot should there be a rebound shot from that side. Indeed, if more feeders are available, then a rebounder can be added (Fig 150 (c)).
   After each delivery the goalkeeper returns to the position of readiness in the centre of the goal. He is working here on *technique* and, although this exercise can be used for fitness training, it is important to decide prior to commencing what the *aim* is as technique will deteriorate as the goalkeeper tires.
   The practice can be used for either leg and both sides should always be included in the programme although not

Fig 149   Practice 3.

164

Fig 150   Practice 4.

(a)

(b)

(c)

(d)

necessarily to the same degree. Remember that if, as is likely, there is just one coach, the 'rebound' element can still be used with skilful sympathetic feeding, e.g. after the initial save and movement into the position of readiness by the post the original feeder can feed a second ball at the far post for a reaction save (Fig 150 (d)).

PRACTICE 5

As for Practice 4, but the coach hits, pushes or slides the ball at the corner. This may be more realistic but requires considerable skill on the part of the feeder. Failure to feed correctly will lead to general frustration!

Fig 151   'It's OK – it has gone wide.' Ian Taylor and Richard Leman keep a close eye on the ball. Seoul Olympics, 1988.

Fig 152   Practice 6.

(a)

(b)

(c)

(d)

(e)

PRACTICE 6 Fig 152
This practice is designed to help the goalkeeper develop his technique of diving effectively (*not spectacularly*) in three stages:

1. The goalkeeper kneels in the centre of the goal with the feeder kneeling about 3m in front of him with a supply of balls (Fig 152 (a)). The feeder feeds to the goalkeeper's left side so that the keeper can dive or roll to save with his left hand. The goalkeeper must not roll onto his stomach, but must dive onto his side so that he is facing the feeder. The idea is for him to use his momentum to regain his kneeling position as quickly as possible. The practice is repeated to the goalkeeper's right side but this time the goalkeeper uses his

left hand or left hand and stick together (Fig 152 (b)). After practice to both sides, the feeder repeats the exercise but this time feeds to alternate sides. (Note that the goalkeeper must always *face* play so that he is aware of where the ball is and can present a barrier for a quick rebound.)
2. The exercise is repeated with the goalkeeper crouching on his haunches (Fig 152 (c)). Note how the hips are thrown at the floor to create a barrier (Fig 152 (d)).
3. The exercise is repeated with the keeper standing (Fig 152 (e)).

PRACTICE 7 Fig 153
This is a continuation of Practice 6 and can be achieved by feeding from the kneeling

position or by accurate flicking.
The goalkeeper stands on the left post while the feeder positions himself just outside the right post, 3m from goal (Fig 153 (a)). The goalkeeper imagines a player advancing towards him from a narrow angle and passing the ball square towards the feeder. On command from the feeder he moves across the goal to save a ball fed from the feeder at about waist height. He has to dive and save the ball with left hand and stick together, maintaining the positions practised in Practice 6 (Fig 152 (b) and (c)). A barrier will be created if the keeper keeps facing play (Fig 153 (d)). The exercise can be repeated on the other post. Increasing the distance of the flick will alter the difficulty of the practice.

Fig 153   Practice 7.

(a)

(b)

(c)

(d)

PRACTICE 8 Fig 154

Practice 7 is repeated with a second ball being fed by the feeder to simulate a rebound after the goalkeeper has regained his position of readiness. Note that the first feeder is out of shot. His position is shown by the balls in the foreground.

Only when these practices have been perfected should the goalkeeper go on to adapt the techniques to play with maximum protection. Maximum protection by its nature restricts movement and can lead to bad habits during the learning process.

Fig 154   Practice 8

Artificial Surface Play and Practice

The basic techniques are the same as those for grass, but are enhanced by the ability to use the *whole body*.

Practices should be aimed at developing technique and improving fitness, speed, and reaction.

Basic Techniques Fig 155

1.   Position of Readiness. Here Ian Taylor shows perfect poise, balance and readiness (Fig 155 (a)).

Fig 155   The basic techniques for artificial surface play.

(a)

(b)

2. When saving, the weight must be *kept forward* so that maximum power and stretch is possible. In Fig 155 (b) Ian Taylor's weight is forward (head over knee, over ankle) as he stretches to save. Note that his eyes are fixed on the ball.

(c)

Fig 155 (c) shows what can happen if the weight is not quite right: the leading leg becomes straight, does not go towards the ball for the save clear and, as clearly illustrated, the shot is harder to save. Ian misses this one by a whisker!

(d)

3. Weight and balance are also important when clearing the ball. Here Ian has just cleared the ball (Fig 155 (d)). Note how balanced he is and how his head is forward, watching intently. The goalkeeper should always be encouraged to go forward.

4. The high shot which has to be saved using the pads is beautifully demonstrated by Veryan Pappin, who has just played the ball. Notice the position of the head and the transfer of weight through the ball (Fig 155 (e)).

(e)

5. The high ball, requiring a hand or hand and stick save needs the same sort of balance and composure. In Fig 155 (f) Ian makes a natural reaction to a ball that is fired at his head or upper body. He loses his balanced position and consequently reduces his chances of saving.

(f)

In Fig 155 (g), however, he is concentrating on keeping himself balanced and is about to save with his left hand.

(g)

In Fig 155 (h) he demonstrates superbly how to take a ball on his right with his left hand coming across. (The striker is Jimmy Kirkwood.)

(h)

6.   Positioning. The goalkeeper must know his angles and the difficulty a forward will have scoring from a narrow angle if he stays his ground and presents a barrier. It is often said of an older, more experienced goalkeeper that he does not have to make spectacular saves because he 'knows where to stand'. Here Ian is ready on his post (Fig 155 (i)). From that position he can effectively save any shot from the angle of approach he is covering or move to intercept a cross. Notice again, his balanced position.

(i)

(j)

In Fig 155 (j) Veryan demonstrates a similar situation. Robert Clift is attacking, shadowed by Paul Barber, while Veryan covers. Providing Veryan stays his ground, there is little danger of Robert scoring. Robert's only option is a pass back or across the circle, but as Fig 155 (k) shows, because Veryan has not committed himself early, he can move to cover the pass.

Analysis of international open play goals shows that most come from situations such as this, and the ability to read the game and move across the goal rapidly to save is an important ability to practise. (Practices 7 and 8 on page 167 will help the goalkeeper move across his goal quickly to dive and block.)

(k)

172

Practices Using Field Players

Clearly, it is necessary to develop technique, together with speed, fitness and reactions, and practices should be made as game-like as possible to promote these improvements.

Remember that practices can be used for different purposes (technique or speed, etc.) but a balanced programme will include sessions designed to develop both. It is not wise to attempt to develop technique when the goalkeeper is tired. Similarly, speedwork and reactions are best practised when the goalkeeper is fairly fresh. A balanced programme would therefore include practices to develop technique, speed and reactions and intensive practices to develop fitness or stamina.

Generally, technique practices should be done slowly with a rest between each while the goalkeeper analyses and discusses with the coach what he is trying to achieve. Speed or reaction practices should be performed quickly in sets of 10–20 shots with a rest between each set. Fitness or stamina practices should be performed until the goalkeeper is very tired before resting.

Each of the following practices can be used to develop any of the three major areas, depending on the rest or intensity pattern that is adopted.

PRACTICE 1 Fig 156
The coach stands outside the circle with a supply of balls. The goalkeeper is in the goal. Two forwards are positioned as in the diagram. The coach feeds the players alternately. They must control the ball and shoot quickly.

PRACTICE 2
As in Practice 1, but a cone is added so that the player has an obstacle to beat.

PRACTICE 3
The coach now feeds the ball further into the circle for the player to run onto. The goalkeeper must find the most appropriate response to the situation. The alternatives include either to come out to the player or stay back, or to stand and await the shot or smother the ball.

The quality of the pass into the space between shooter and goalkeeper is crucial to the success of this practice. Coaches must develop their personal skill in this area.

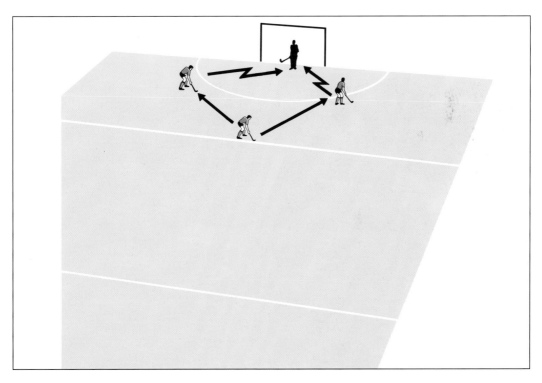

Fig 156   Practice 1.

PRACTICE 4 Fig 157
As in Practice 3, but the goalkeeper (John Hurst) creates a barrier on his left to smother a forward (Keith Rowley) coming through with the ball (Fig 157 (a)–(c)). The player is fed a square ball and has to attack the circle and go round the goalkeeper on the goalkeeper's left side. The goalkeeper attempts to channel the player and times his forward movement to meet the player.

A defender can be added to the player's left to force him to the goalkeeper's left side. The practice should be adapted so that the player may shoot and the goalkeeper learn to read the shot and place his body behind it.

The principal coaching points are:

1. The position of the goalkeeper's body must create as large a barrier as possible.

Fig 157   Practice 4.

(a)

2. The position of the head must always face the ball. Fig 157 (d) shows the head flung back, thus obstructing vision.
3. The position of the reverse stick must allow for a reverse stick tackle to be made, as in Fig 157 (e)–(g).

Study carefully the movement of body, arms and stick to provide a wide and effective barrier.

Fig 158   Stephen Batchelor driving past Volter Fried of West Germany in the 1988 Olympics.

(b)

(c)

(d)

(e)

(f)

(g)

Fig 159   Practice 5.

(a)

(b)

(c)

PRACTICE 5 Fig 159
As in Practice 4, but to the goalkeeper's right. (Fig 159 (a)–(c)).

PRACTICE 6 Fig 160
Practice 4 can now be repeated with the forward attacking and going round either side of the goalkeeper or shooting as the goalkeeper advances with a defender added to aid the goalkeeper as necessary.

The feeder on the right feeds the ball to the forward. The opposite defender moves as the forward receives the ball. The forward then attacks the circle.

The goalkeeper has to 'read' the situation and decide whether to attack the forward or stay his ground. The defender chases back. It is important that goalkeeper and defender communicate with each other.

PRACTICE 7
As in Practice 1, but two more players are added as 'rebounders'.

Practised indoors or outdoors with tennis balls or light to normal hockey balls, the coach feeds a player at the top of the circle. The player shoots *at* the goalkeeper, who aims to save clear *to* one of the other players, who in turn attempts to shoot. This helps the goalkeeper to learn to save in a controlled fashion. The ball is kept in play as long as possible. This is also an extremely good practice for forwards.

The coach can easily make the practice more competitive by increasing the tempo. The players shoot quickly and accurately, the goalkeeper attempts to clear the circle safely and the rebounders attempt to rebound. A variety of scores can be kept, the players attempting to score more goals than each other

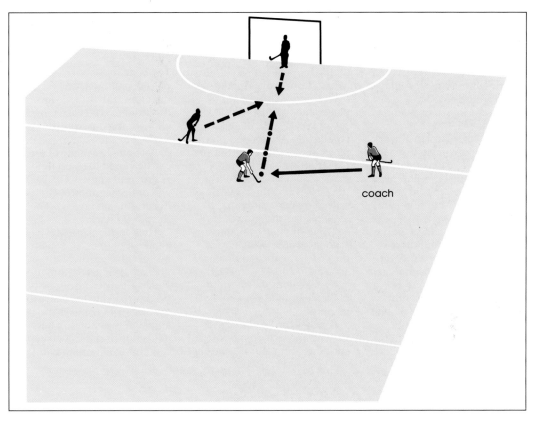

Fig 160   Practice 6.

while the goalkeeper attempts to clear the circle each time. The total number of goals scored can be used as a competition between goalkeeper and goalkeeper, and players and goalkeeper, and so on.

After the competitive element has been introduced, the coach can bring in a defender to help the goalkeeper. In this situation the coach must apply strict safety rules, penalizing dangerous play immediately.

Clearly, the practices are gradually becoming more game-like and involving other members of the team, who are also practising specific skills related to their position.

PRACTICE 8
This practice develops the speed of reaction in both the goalkeeper and the striker.

Here the coach starts with a supply of balls on the goal-line about 5m from one of the goalposts. The goalkeeper stands in the goal by the post nearest to the coach. Three to five players stand in the circle about 7–14m from the goal. The coach feeds a ball to one of the players who has to control and flick, push or hit the ball at goal quickly. If he is near to the goal, the player should flick the ball; if he is further away, he should hit it. The goalkeeper must judge whether to stay his ground or advance and smother the shot.

PRACTICE 9
A defender can be added to make the practice more game-like and competitive. This will increase the pressure on the striker to shoot quickly.

At this point it is worth mentioning the Basic Techniques again. The goalkeeper must concentrate on keeping his weight forward. If he decides to smother the shot, then again he must face the ball as he advances to create a good barrier.

A significant proportion of goals at all levels are scored by players moving on to crosses played across the face of the goal. It is therefore important for the goalkeeper to be able to react to these situations and Practices 10 and 11 show how the coach can simulate this in basic technique practices.

PRACTICE 10
The goalkeeper stands covering the left post. A player advances toward the goalkeeper from a narrow angle and plays the ball backward of square to one or more players coming in on the far post. The goalkeeper must quickly readjust position by moving across the goal and judging whether to stand and save, or smother the shot.

This is good practice for the attacking players but there is considerable opportunity for error. The coach must judge whether the players are able to do this practice sufficiently well for the goalkeeper to gain real benefit. If they are not then the coach should employ the next practice.

PRACTICE 11 Fig 161
This practice is set up as for Practice 9 but only one extra player is needed, positioned on the far post with a supply of balls. The first player moves in from a narrow angle and passes the ball toward the second player. As the ball passes him, the second player plays his shot from his supply of stationary balls (a third player can be used to collect the passes and thus save time retrieving the balls later).

By using extra ground equipment often available in schools or at Sports Centres, the coach can extend practices such as 11 and 12 to make them game-like without extending his often limited personnel resources.

Benches can be placed at varying angles to a goal post such that a shot outside the goal

will rebound toward goal to test the reactions of the goalkeeper.

PRACTICE 12
The benches or boxes are placed as shown, one on top of the other, the flat side facing the striker. The striker shoots either at the goal directly or at the box to simulate a deflection. The angle of the box can be varied to simulate shots at different angles. The balls will deflect at different angles, depending on which part of the box it hits.

The coach encourages the goalkeeper to react, staying on his feet and putting into practice the basic techniques already learned. After he has become used to the practice, the angle of the boxes can be adjusted to simulate a far post deflection and the goalkeeper can dive to save with hand or

Fig 161   Practice 11.

stick. Obviously, there are any number of variations that can be added. For example, more boxes can be added and shots can be hit from both sides of the goal.

To gain maximum benefit from the practice the goalkeeper must not 'creep' across the goal towards the deflection. He can be kept in line by the striker shooting at his near post rather than at the box.

Defending Penalty Corners

Before the revolution in penalty corner goalkeeping techniques during the last few years, the majority of goalkeepers advanced from the goal-line to a distance of 1–5m, stood up and relied on their reactions to save conventionally. This should *still* be learned and practised before other techniques are employed. The Russians, Germans and gradually the rest of the hockey-playing nations have now adopted the charging or 'dropping' technique which has evolved since the rule change of 1989.

The rule change was formulated in order to curb the practice employed by some goalkeepers, particularly on the Continent, of 'logging'. 'Logging' means the goalkeeper going down 'like a log' *before* any shot has been made. In England better goalkeepers have attempted to react to the shot, going down with it, to actively save it with hand, stick or body, and it seems this will still be allowed.

Thus there are three main methods of saving penalty corners under the rules as they now stand: standing, going down to save and charging, indoor style. Of these, the latter is the least used.

Standing

This is the method used by all goalkeepers until the late 1970s. It should be used by *all* goalkeepers except at the highest level as it requires the ultimate in skill and reaction. It should be used as basic training for all young goalkeepers. It can invariably be used on grass.

PRINCIPAL COACHING POINTS
1. The distance the goalkeeper moves off his line will vary depending on the size of the goalkeeper and his reaction time. Generally, a shorter goalkeeper will need to move further off his line than a taller goalkeeper in order to narrow the angle. The taller goalkeeper will have a longer reach and perhaps minutely slower reactions.
2. Two full backs may be necessary, one on either post. The full back on the goalkeeper's left will have to come level with the goalkeeper in order to cover both the post *and* the vulnerable area toward the defensive left top of the *circle*.
3. If the ball is moved past the 'runner-out' it may be necessary for the goalkeeper to charge and smother any shot, or the player on the left post may be able to reach the ball. Obviously, the defence of corners using this technique requires considerable practice and understanding.
4. The goalkeeper must be in a position of readiness *before* the shot from the top of the circle.
5. Remember that it is important to balance reaction time with the distance from the line to narrow the angle.

Going Down to Save

Technically, this implies that

the goalkeeper can go down to block *as the ball is hit*. Studying video footage of Ian Taylor at the 1984 Olympics and 1986 World Cup, it is evident that he tried to do this from the early days of the technique.

Thus, in developing this technique, the coach must instil in the goalkeeper the need to *react to the ball*. The goalkeeper must advance quickly from the line to a distance of about 4–5m, coming to rest with the weight on the outside of the right foot, and inside of the left. His body will be leaning to the right. The goalkeeper will drop to the right as the ball is struck. The exact position of the feet will depend upon at which post the goalkeeper prefers to have the covering defender. The aim should be to use the *left hand* to save as much as possible, preferably *trapping* the ball for the defender on the goalkeeper's left to clear.

COACHING POINTS Fig 162
1. The goalkeeper must aim to get his head behind the line of the ball (Fig 162 (a)).
2. The goalkeeper must aim to save with his left hand or right hand and stick (together on his right side). If the ball is to the goalkeeper's left he should still aim to use the left hand for control even in front of the legs. Using the hand in this way will enable the goalkeeper to get the head as near to the line of the ball as possible as well as adding control (Fig 162 (b)).
3. The goalkeeper must react to the shot. While it is important to react when the ball is struck rather than before, if a dummy forces the goalkeeper down early, no foul is committed if the ball is then struck, that is the goalkeeper can remain down.
4. By thinking 'hand' the goalkeeper will tend to react to

179

Fig 162   Going down to save.

(a)

(b)

Fig 163   Practice 1.

(a)

(b)

(c)

(c)

the shot and go down actively as a barrier to block the shot, rather than just going down.

5.   The goalkeeper should then be encouraged to create a barrier on his side rather than dive onto his stomach (Fig 162 (c)).

Progressive Practices for Going Down to Save

PRACTICE 1 Fig 163
The goalkeeper lays on his right side 4–5m from the line, as shown also in Fig 162 (c). His legs cover the left post (if appropriate), as if having gone down to block a shot. His body should be bent at the waist, weight supported on the right-hand stick or the elbow with the left hand raised poised to save (Fig 162 (b)). The feeder stands with a supply of balls, preferably light training balls (not wind balls) or tennis balls.

The feeder strikes a ball for the goalkeeper to save with his left hand, or left or right-hand stick, etc. Obviously, the feeder hits softly to start with, building up pace as the goalkeeper becomes more proficient (Fig 163 (a)). The feeder should also concentrate on areas the goalkeeper finds difficult, e.g. just over the waist, the legs, to the goalkeeper's right for a full extension stick save, etc., as in Fig 163 (b). If the ball is going toward the lower legs, the goalkeeper should save with his legs or feet. However, reacting with his hand will make a save with his feet or legs more controlled, as his head will be moving toward the ball (Fig 163 (c)).

Fig 164   Practice 2.

Fig 165   Practice 3.

Fig 166   Practice 5.

PRACTICE 2 Fig 164
Practice 1 is repeated, but starts with the goalkeeper kneeling. He leans slightly right, left hand raised, as he reacts to the shot. He must be encouraged to form a barrier as he goes down, making sure his legs cover the left post.

PRACTICE 3 Fig 165
The goalkeeper progresses from kneeling to squatting on his haunches to standing, leaning right each time.

PRACTICE 4
The goalkeeper runs out, sets himself and then the feeder shoots, having watched to ensure the goalkeeper is stationary and leaning right, with left hand ready.

PRACTICE 5 Fig 166
It is important to note that the entire movement of going down tends to force the goalkeeper right and, if the aim is to cover the left post with the feet, then the goalkeeper must line up slightly left of the centre of the goal before running out. There is no reason why the goalkeeper should not attempt to cover the right post, with a defender to his left, but remember that it is harder for the defender on the line to the goalkeeper's left to see the shot as it comes through the runner out and past the goalkeeper.

A second feeder can simulate a stick stop by standing outside the circle with arm raised, hand holding a ball. He should advance into the circle about two to three paces and place the ball for the striker. The goalkeeper should move as the stopper brings his arm down (this should be his first movement). The coach will need to adjust the timing of the stopper to make the practice as realistic as possible.

182

PRACTICE 6

The coach can now progress to a full defensive routine. The goalkeeper A, lined up a little left, runs 4–5m out, sets himself and reacts to the shot, making sure his legs and feet cover his left post if he drops to the lying position.

The first player out runs in such a way as to be able to veer off if the ball is slipped either way. The left post player comes out to level or just behind the goalkeeper's feet in order to clear off the pads or hand, the goalkeeper having controlled the ball. This player must also cover the circle ahead and to the left.

The line player, slightly in from the post, covers the area to the goalkeeper's right. The player to the right of the goal is ready to cover the save to the goalkeeper's extreme right and clear, block runners into the penalty spot area, and cover the right side of the circle.

Charging Indoor Style

This method of saving leaves the goalkeeper vulnerable to the slip to right or left, but it is a useful weapon as a variation. It also has the advantage of creating a high offside line.

PRINCIPAL COACHING POINTS
1.   The goalkeeper runs as far and as fast as possible and goes down to smother as the ball is hit.
2.   The goalkeeper creates as large a barrier as possible, by smothering on his side, keeping his eyes on the shot at all times.
3.   Turning his head away (a natural reaction) will lead to him turning, landing on his stomach, rolling and exposing an unprotected side or back to the shot! It will also lower his 'barrier'!
4.   The defence can be the same as for the previous technique in Practice 6 but it is more effective to run a 'wedge' with a defender on either side of the goalkeeper to provide cover.

13

DEVELOPING YOUNG PLAYERS

A coach needs to foster a young player's curiosity and interest through exploration, experimentation and discovery to encourage decision-makers. To enable young players to learn effectively, the coach needs to have an appreciation of:

1. How young players learn.
2. The characteristics of different age groups, including their physical and social development.
3. Structure and style of a coaching session.
4. The technical and tactical knowledge players already possess, which involves the ability to observe, evaluate and assess.

Young players learn by participating actively, having fun, being motivated, being challenged, and achieving success. Players who feel good about themselves produce good results. The successful coach will consider these points when planning a programme and working with young players. While ensuring progression and development, beginning with what the players already know and understand, the coach also needs to help young players to:

1. Develop confidence in fundamental techniques.
2. Understand fundamental concepts and tactics in team play.
3. Cope with competition.
4. Understand the rules of the game.
5. Develop sportsmanship.

Warm Up/Warm Down

Experience has shown that while both senior and junior players appreciate the need for a well-structured warm up, players still generally need to be educated further in understanding the importance of a warm down after every session.

The important characteristics that coaches should recognize include the following.

Under 10s and 12s

1. While girls may be physiologically ahead of boys, their strength is similar and so they should be coached together.
2. These young players are enthusiastic, highly motivated, and particularly the under 10s are egocentric and like to be involved with the ball.
3. They enjoy being active and learn by participating.
4. Fine motor coordination is still at an elementary level, while their technical ability is such that greater emphasis should be on activities involving large body movements.
5. Physical and social development are appropriate to individual and small group work, with no more than five, six or seven a side on quarter to half a pitch.
6. This age group enjoys scoring goals, so there should be plenty of opportunity with, for example, no circles or wider goals.
7. Ability to concentrate is limited, while self-esteem is of prime importance. Sessions should therefore be between 45 minutes and one hour, with a variety of exciting, active and challenging activities giving all children the opportunity to achieve.
8. Because young players are motivated by achieving success, competition should be kept to a minimum with activities focusing on developing fundamental techniques and concepts of team play.
9. Observation skills are fairly limited; demonstrations must be clear, simple and at a pace that a few key points can be highlighted, seen and understood.

Grid Systems

A grid is a most valuable facility since it acts as a ready-made organization for grouping young players, as well as giving ready defined playing areas for team play.

A grid can easily be marked out on a playground, grass area, or hockey pitch using chalk, cones, bibs or skittles and can be anything from 5–10m squares, or 10 × 12½m on a pitch.

Under 14s

While many of the points relating to the under 10s and 12s also apply to the under 14s, the coach also needs to recognize the following:

1. Boys are becoming physically stronger at this stage, so that it *may* be preferable for boys and girls to be coached separately. However, this depends on the specific stages of development since they may continue to benefit from playing together.
2. Fine motor coordination is developing, so that the players' ability to cope with greater technical and tactical details means activities can be more demanding and competitive, advancing from seven-a-side team play on half a pitch to eleven a side on a full pitch.
3. Increased ability to concentrate allows sessions to be planned for between one hour and one and a half hours.

Structure and Style of a Coaching Session

No matter what structure or style the coach chooses, all sessions should address the following general principles:

1. Overall aims of the programme.
2. Short-term objectives of the individual session.
3. Length and structure of session.
4. Available space and equipment.
5. Number of players and coaches.
6. Fun and enjoyment.
7. Developing decision-makers.
8. Attitude of the coach: enthusiastic, friendly, patient, sense of humour, firm but fair.
9. Gradual introduction of pressure.

Gradual Introduction of Pressure

The skill of the coach is to introduce progressive pressure challenging the players while still ensuring there is an opportunity for them to achieve success, which is such an important motivating factor.

Progressive pressure can be introduced by:

1. Reducing the time available.
2. Reducing the space available.
3. Competition against self.
4. Competition team vs team.
5. Competition individual vs individual.

However, with young players the degree of competition should be appropriate to maintain *enjoyment* and *success*.

---

10. At all times the coach needs to *watch, listen, question* and *praise*.

Historically, coaches have emphasized learning a skill and then developing this into a game situation, where the tendency appears to have been to instruct the players on exactly what is to be done. More recently, other models of coaching have developed where the emphasis has moved towards games making and understanding through games, where the coach acts as a facilitator, fostering the curiosity and interest of players through exploration, experimentation and discovery, encouraging them to find out for themselves and solve problems, thus developing into decision-makers.

In order to achieve their maximum potential it is ideal

COACHING MODEL 1
Skill → Game
Strengths
1. Clarity in understanding the skill.   2. Easier for the coach to plan in advance.   3. Minimum opportunity for behaviour problems as little communication between players.
Points to be aware of
1. Coach directed.   2. Difficulties in motivating some players to practise skills effectively in isolation.   3. Difficulties in advancing from doing the skill to using the skill, i.e. little opportunity to develop decison-making.   4. Little opportunity to develop social interaction so crucial to successful team play.   5. Greater opportunity for players to fail, i.e. some children will never be able to execute the skill, while others will learn an isolated skill out of context.

COACHING MODEL 2
Game → Skill → Game

Strengths

1. Players highly motivated to practise a skill effectively, appreciating the need to learn the skill.
2. Players develop an understanding of when to use the skill in a game.
3. Development of problem-solving and decision-making skills.
4. Player-centred model – the coach is able to begin with what the players know.
5. Opportunities for social interaction. Players are involved in their own learning, share ideas and work co-operatively.
6. Emphasis on teaching the players rather than teaching the skill.
7. Opportunities for players to develop skills of observation.

Points to be aware of

1. Be flexible and adapt plans according to the response from players, to be able to alter games and practices accordingly.
2. Watch, listen and ask questions, being aware that coach intervention may inhibit some of the decision-making and problem-solving.
3. Greater opportunity arises for disagreements and take-over by dominant individuals. Players unused to this model often initially find it difficult to co-operate effectively. However, with time there is a change in attitude as players become actively involved.
4. More time is needed to allow players the opportunity to explore, experiment, discover, plan and evaluate.

COACHING MODEL 3
Games making → Skill → Game

Strengths

1. All the strengths listed under model 2.
2. Players can begin to be responsible for choosing rules, methods of start/restart, ways of scoring, etc., thus developing an appreciation of rules.

Points to be aware of

1. All those under model 2.
2. Constraints due to available resources.

to encourage young players to be decision-makers, to understand fundamental concepts and to be able to solve problems as they arise in matches. Coaching models 2 and 3 are therefore favoured, while model 1 may also be included when time to work with a group is minimal, for example in a shortened course, or when a squad has a tournament in which to play. However, even with model 1 it is preferable that the coach uses a more player-centred approach asking questions starting with *what, how, when,* and *where*.

With young players, questions need to be simple and focus the attention on only one or two points at a time.

The following example (Fig 167) of a simple practice developing the push pass gives possible questions the coach might ask. Note the simple questions for young players:

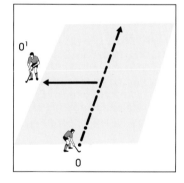

Fig 167 Developing the push pass.

What are you trying to do with the ball?
Pass it to O^1.
How are you trying to pass the ball to O^1?
Along the ground.
When are you trying to pass the ball?
When O^1 asks for it.

How do you know when O[1] wants the ball?
When he calls for it.
How else could O[1] show you when to pass?
When he puts his stick on the ground.
Where are you aiming to send the ball?
To O[1]'s stick.
How can O[1] help you know where to pass the ball?
By putting his stick on the ground.

The programmes that follow serve to illustrate activities appropriate to the under 10s, under 12s and under 14s with consideration paid to how young players learn; characteristics of the different age groups; structure and style of coaching sessions; and observation, evaluation and assessment to guide planning and ensure progression and development both through a single session and from session to session.

All three programmes have a common theme of *passing and receiving*. Coaches will appreciate the need to repeat activities through subsequent sessions when the need arises, as well as that other techniques and concepts of team play will need to be developed as they are recognized by players and coaches. Other chapters in the book will give suggestions on other areas of play.

Session 1 (Under 10s)

PRACTICE 1
Objectives To move with the ball and during the warm up to introduce players to dribbling techniques.
Procedure Each player has a ball and they dribble wherever they wish in a restricted area avoiding one another.

PRACTICE 2
Objectives To introduce the push pass straight ahead from

a stationary position and receiving from in front.
Procedure Players pass through the cones.

With insufficient equipment it is suggested that after passing, the player follows the ball and joins the end of the other line.

Progressive pressure
Counting how many passes are made in one minute and seeing how long it takes each pair or team to make ten to twenty passes.

Possible questions to develop the push pass that can be asked are:

How can you send the ball?
Is it easier to send the ball fast with your hands together on the stick or apart?
Is it easier to stand sideways to the goal or facing it?
How can you make the ball travel faster?

Experiment with the follow-through after you have passed the ball. Is your pass more accurate when the stick head follows through towards the goal?

PRACTICE 3
Objectives To introduce passing to the left and receiving from the right, and to develop pace in passing.
Procedure Four players pass the ball clockwise round the grid while another player sprinting around the outside of the grid aims to beat the ball home.

PRACTICE 4 (ROLLER CRICKET) Fig 168
Objectives To develop pace and vision moving with the ball; pace and accuracy in passing to the left; and receiving from the right.
Procedure The coach may

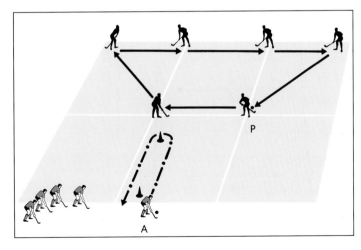

Fig 168   Practice 4.

find it useful to introduce this game through roller cricket – the ball is rolled rather than using a hockey stick and ball. Once the players understand the game, the more complicated technique of using a hockey stick can be introduced.

Players form teams of five, six or seven in six grids and use two balls.

On 'go' the first batsman moves with the ball around the two cones. Each return to the start counts as a rounder or goal. At the same time the fielding team begins passing clockwise to the fielders at cones. The next batsman takes over when the fielders' ball returns to the batting team.

Progressive pressure
Recording the total rounders or goals scored by the batting team after players have had one or two turns each and then letting teams change over. Make the run a figure eight.

Possible questions to achieve the objectives are:

How can the fielders make the ball travel faster?
How can the fielders pass the ball more accurately?
How can the batsmen move more quickly with the ball?
Is it easier when the ball is near the batsmen's feet or well out in front?

It is useful to use this first session to assess the development and understanding of players to guide subsequent detailed planning.

Session 2 (Under 10s)

PRACTICE 1 Fig 169
Objectives   To develop pace and accuracy in the push pass.
Procedure   Players pass through the cones.

With insufficient equipment players work in teams.

Progressive pressure
Counting how many passes are made in one minute and challenging players to beat their own scores; seeing who is the first pair or team to make ten passes through the cones; increasing the distance the ball has to travel, reducing the distance between the cones, and passing two balls simultaneously through a wider goal.

PRACTICE 2 Fig 170
Objectives   To introduce passing to the left on the move and moving after making a pass.
Procedure O^1 dribbles to the middle and passes left, continuing on to the opposite side of the grid.

Possible questions to pose accompany Fig 167.

With insufficient equipment players work in teams.
Progressive pressure
Counting how many passes

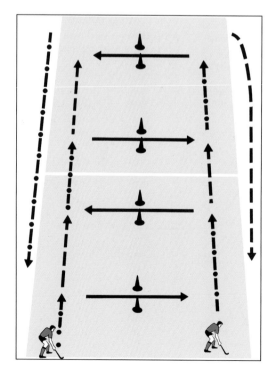

Fig 169   Practice 1.

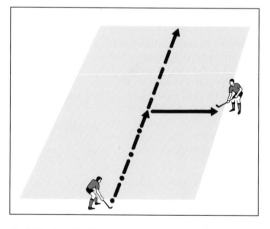

Fig 170   Practice 2.

188

are made in one minute and seeing who is the first pair or team to make ten to twenty passes.

PRACTICE 3 (ROLLER CRICKET)

Objectives   To provide opportunity to further develop pace and vision moving with the ball; pace and accuracy in passing to the left while stationary and moving; and receiving from the right.

Procedure   Repeat the game as in Practice 4, Session 1, possibly introducing it again through roller cricket. When player technique allows, fielders should dribble to the next cone and pass. Passing on the move should be encouraged.

Session 3 (Under 10s)

PRACTICE 1

Objectives   To introduce passing to the right while moving and moving after making a pass.

Procedure   O[1] dribbles to the middle and passes to the right, continuing onto the opposite side of the grid.

With insufficient equipment players work in teams.

Progressive pressure Counting how many passes are made in one minute and seeing who is the first pair or team to make ten to twenty passes.

Possible questions to develop during passing to the right on the move are:

How can a player pass to the right without first stopping the ball?
Is it easier to pass when the ball is in front of the right foot or behind?
How can a player get the ball behind his right foot?

PRACTICE 2

Objectives   To develop pace

in passing to the right and to introduce receiving from the left.

Procedure   Four players pass the ball anticlockwise round the grid while another player sprinting around the outside of the grid aims to beat the ball home.

PRACTICE 3 (ROLLER CRICKET)

Objectives   To provide opportunity to further develop pace and vision moving with the ball; pace and accuracy in passing to the right while stationary and moving; and receiving from the left.

Procedure   Repeat the game as in Practice 4, Session 1, with fielders passing anticlockwise first in a stationary position, then dribbling to the next cone and passing while moving. Batsmen can slalom dribble or move using Indian dribble.

Session 4 (Under 10s)

PRACTICE 1

Objectives   To develop understanding of where and when to pass and receiving while moving from the left and right.

Procedure   With insufficient equipment players work in teams.

PRACTICE 2

Objectives   To develop vision in passing as to when and where to pass and to move to receive a pass.

Procedure   Four players in a grid pass in sequence. What signal tells them when and where to pass? What signal tells them when and where to move to receive a pass?

PRACTICE 3

Objectives   To develop fundamental concepts of passing to maintain possession while under pressure and where and when to support

the player in possession.

Procedure   3 vs 1. The batting team aims to maintain possession, while the fielding team aims to intercept and pass the ball out of the grid.

Progressive pressure   The fielding team can progress from only closing down and not tackling to tackling.

Possible questions to achieve the objectives are:

Where can support players move to make it easier to give a successful pass?
Square to the player in possession.
When is it best to move to receive a pass?
When the receiver has control of the ball.
What signal helps to tell you the player with the ball is ready to pass?
Eye contact.
What can you do if you are closed down by the defender?
Pretend to pass one way and then pass the other.

Session 5 (Under 10s)

PRACTICE 1

Objectives   To further develop vision in passing, when and where to pass and move to receive a pass.

Procedure   Repeat Practice 2, Session 4, with two groups in one grid.

Progressive pressure Reducing the available space.

PRACTICE 2

Objectives   To further develop passing to maintain possession while under pressure and to support the player in possession.

Procedure   3 vs 1 as in Practice 3, Session 4.

Progressive pressure Increased pace of pass; dummy passes to make it more difficult for the defender; and using flat or low lifted passes.

The players and coach may recognize the need to practise

the techniques of giving and receiving a low lifted pass, while the coach may also impose the condition of no tackling to allow success in using this pass.

PRACTICE 3 (PAIR PASSING)
Objectives   To develop vision in passing using eye contact and passing and receiving while moving both with a flat pass and a low lifted pass.
Procedure   Eight to ten players in four grids, each with a ball. Players move about the grid, aiming to exchange their ball with another player. Consecutive passes to the same player are not allowed.
Progressive pressure
Counting how many passes are made in one minute and seeing who is the first player to make ten passes.

Session 6 (Under 10s)

PRACTICE 1
Objectives   To develop passing to maintain possession; to beat a defender; to create scoring chances; to develop support to the player in possession; and to introduce basic defending strategies (intercept, delay, close down,

---

Under 12s
If the under 12s have not worked on an introductory programme on passing and receiving, the programme for the under 10s can be explored. However, if they have experienced such a programme they can be challenged further. Possible areas of work might include:

1.   Review of previous work.
2.   Introduction to the reverse stick push.
3.   Developing passing square to left and right.
4.   Introduction to the use of dummy passes (disguised passes) and using the low lifted pass.
5.   Creating 2 vs 1 and 3 vs 2.

---

channel, reduce options).
Procedure   3 vs 1. The attackers score by dribbling over one end line of a pitch 10 × 5m while the defender scores by gaining possession and passing over the other end line.

The coach should help players recognize the need to practise certain fundamental techniques as and when appropriate for the success of this game.

PRACTICE 2
Objectives   To develop passing and receiving as explored through the six sessions.
Procedure   Introducing 3 vs 3

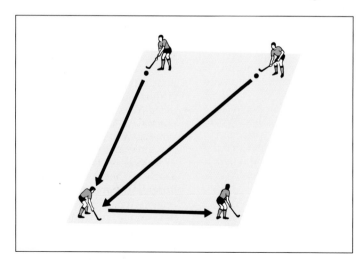

Fig 171   Practice 3.

---

and 4 vs 4 in four grids. There should be plenty of opportunity to score goals by dribbling over an end line, scoring through a wide goal (no circles) and scoring by passing to a team member through any of four goals inside the playing area.
Progressive pressure
Developing to 5 vs 5, 6 vs 6 and 7 vs 7 on a quarter to half pitch; introducing hitting, using longer and harder passes; and developing aerial passing.

Session 1 (Under 12s)

PRACTICE 1
Objectives   To develop pace in the push pass and receiving in a ready position to make the next pass.

Procedure   There are four players to a grid. Two players diagonally opposite each other each have a ball. Players must aim to get both balls with one player, passing clockwise or anticlockwise.

PRACTICE 2
Objectives   To develop passing to maintain possession while under pressure and support to the player in possession.
Procedure   4 vs 2. Where could the supporting players move to help the player with the ball? When is it best to

move to help support the player with the ball?

Progressive pressure   The defenders (fielding team) proceed from only closing down to tackling. While the four attackers aim to maintain possession, the two defenders aim to touch the ball to gain a point. Defenders work as a unit to limit passing options. Attackers use low lifted passes to avoid defenders' sticks and dummy passes.

To develop the low lifted pass when appropriate, some of the practices for the under 10s can be used.

PRACTICE 3 (ROLLER BALL)

Objectives   To develop concepts of team play in passing to maintain possession, spatial awareness and movement of supporting players.

Procedure   Two teams of five, six or seven a side in four grids. Players can pass the ball only by rolling. If the ball goes out of the grids, it is a free roll to the opposition. The consecutive passes must be counted by one team before the opposition gain possession.

The player with the ball can move but the emphasis is on the other players in the team moving to receive the ball. The team selected to commence the game should start by rolling the ball to one of their own team. The opposition gain possession by intercepting the pass.

PRACTICE 4 (CONSECUTIVE HOCKEY)

This can be played when the players' technical and tactical ability is of a level to cope with the increased demands of the game.
Objectives   Same as for Practice 3.
Procedure   Players use a hockey stick and ball. The rules

are the same as for roller ball and with no tackling. The opposition gain possession as in roller ball by intercepting the pass.
Progressive pressure
Introducing tackling.

Session 2 (Under 12s)

PRACTICE 1

Objectives   To develop an understanding of when and where to pass and move after making a pass.
Procedure O^1 passes to O^2, then moves diagonally to the opposite side of the grid. O^2 passes to O^1 at a new place and runs diagonally, that is the ball travels around the grid while the players move diagonally across the grid.

Repeat with the ball travelling anticlockwise.

PRACTICE 2

Objectives   To develop passing and receiving under pressure and vision when passing.
Procedure   There are four players and three balls in a grid. O^2 passes to O^1 who receives and passes back to O^2.

This should be repeated with O^3 and O^4 in sequence.
Progressive pressure
Reducing the time delay between O^1 receiving one ball and the next and seeing who is first to complete twenty passes.

PRACTICE 3 Fig 171

Objectives   To develop passing and receiving under pressure and vision when passing.
Procedure   There are four players and two balls in a grid. O^2 passes to O^1 who receives and passes to the free player.

This should be repeated for twenty passes. As players become more skilful the practice can be made more challenging. How?

PRACTICE 4 (CONSECUTIVE HOCKEY) – WITH TACKLING

Objectives   Same as for Practice 3, Session 2.
Procedure   Same as for Practice 4, Session 2, but with tackling.

Session 3 (Under 12s)

PRACTICE 1

Objectives   To develop using a square pass to the left and right and receiving in a ready position to make the next pass; and to introduce goal scoring.
Procedure   With the ball on the left, O^1 or O^2 square passes through cones, finishing with a shot at goal.

This should be repeated, beginning with the ball on the right.

When necessary, the individual skills for this game should be practised to be successful, e.g. receiving outside the right foot from left and right; shooting with a drive or short back lift; and flicking, pushing, squeezing and slapping rebound shots.
Progressive pressure   Feeding two balls for rebound shots by O^3 and including goalkeepers.

Possible questions to achieve the objectives are:

Where is it easier for the player to receive the ball in order to continue travelling forward at pace – from the right or left? Where does the pass need to be made so the receiver can continue moving forward without stopping?
When does the receiver need to move forward in order to receive on the move?
What kind of shot is best – for shooting from the top of the circle; for rebound shots?

PRACTICE 2

Objectives   To develop moving to receive the next pass; receiving from the right; shooting and rebounds.

Procedure A player passes to and receives from a line of players on his way from the half-way line, finishing with a shot.
Progressive pressure The coach feeds the ball for rebound work and goalkeepers can be involved.

PRACTICE 3

Objectives To develop fundamental techniques of passing and receiving and concepts of passing to beat a defender; team play; 2 vs 1 attacking options; passing to create scoring opportunities; and passing to maintain possession.
Procedure Developing 2 vs 1 and using goals, the attackers score by dribbling over the end line of a pitch 15 x 10m. The defender scores by gaining possession and passing over the other end line.
Progressive pressure
Throughout these activities fundamental concepts of defence in team play can be developed alongside the attacking concepts. An extra defender can be added after a predetermined number of seconds.
Note Adjust time before the defender joins in, according to the technical and tactical ability of the players.

Possible questions to achieve objectives for 2 vs 1 might include:

Attackers (2) Which is the easiest way of beating the defender in order to create a scoring opportunity – by passing or dribbling round him? **Note** The defender can help by saying what makes it easier or more difficult for him. How can the defender be committed, making space for the receiver?
Is it easier to beat the defender when passing to his stick side or his non-stick side?
Where is it therefore better for

Under 14s

Providing the fundamental work as suggested for the under 10s and under 12s has been covered, possible developments might include:

1. Review of previous work.
2. Attacking patterns, that is where players and the ball are trying to get to.
3. More complex decision-making by increasing options.

---

the player with the ball to have the support?
If passing from left to right, where does the receiver need to be in relation to the defender so that the defender is easily beaten by the pass and cannot tackle back?
Defenders Where does the defender prefer the ball – with the player on the left or right? If the ball is with the player on the right, how can the defender get it over to the left?

Possible Activities (Under 14s)

PRACTICE 1 (3 VS 2)
Objectives To develop fundamental techniques and concepts of team play when defending, and in passing and receiving when attacking.
Procedure As 2 vs 1 for under 12s above.
Progressive pressure
Reducing time to score and adding an extra defender after a short time.

Possible questions to achieve objectives might include:

Attackers (3) Where is it best to have the ball so there are more options and it is therefore easier to create scoring chances?
If the ball is with an outside player, how can the players get it into the middle?
Where are the attackers trying to get the ball?
Is it easier for the defenders if the ball is kept in the same channel, or moved quickly?
Where do the defenders not want a free player?

Defenders (2) Where do the defenders prefer the ball to be? How can they get it or keep it there?
What do they want to force the player with the ball to do?

PRACTICE 3 (3 VS 2)

Objectives As in Practice 1, but developing the understanding of fundamental techniques and concepts in team play both defending and attacking in 3 vs 2 in specific areas of the field.
Procedure Attacking the top of the circle and using a goalkeeper.
Progressive pressure Adding a third defender after limited time to increase pace of attack and allowing defenders to gain possession and pass over 25yd line.

PRACTICE

Objectives Creating space to receive a pass and understanding when and where to pass.
Procedure The centre back passes to the right half. The right wing times a run moving infield then out, creating more options than remaining near the side line. If the left half moves infield, the right half passes to the right wing's reverse stick.
If the left half stays near the side line, the right half plays the ball for the right wing to receive infield on the open side.

When the players and coach recognize that the practice falls down through lack of

Fig 172   Sean Kerly, a fine example for young players to follow, shows here the intense concentration required at the highest level.

Watching	What? Narrow focus, e.g. passing – look at body position, grip, preparation, action, follow-through and pace.
Listening	To players while they are working. To answers to questions.
Questioning	To develop understanding and consequently players who are decision-makers.

technique, the appropriate technique should be worked on before returning to the pattern of play.

Possible questions to create these options:

Where does the left half *not* want the right wing or the ball? How can the right wing move to create more options? When should the right wing move infield? What if the left half moves infield to mark the right wing? What if the left half stays near the side line? What kind of pass must the right half give? How, where and when?

PRACTICE 4
Objectives   To develop Practice 3 to 3 vs 2.
Procedure   Players work to create the same pattern as in Practice 3. How? If the left wing shuts out the right half what can the right half do? Where can he move?

When does the right wing move? What must the passes between the centre back and

right half be like to make it difficult for the left wing?

Observation, Evaluation and Assessment

Historically, because coaching was pre-planned and often 'coach directed', assessment of the needs and abilities of players was sometimes ignored. The most effective . coach will use an initial session with players to assess the level of their hockey knowledge, both technical and tactical.

Working with young players can be exciting, challenging and most rewarding to those coaches who understand the differences in working with young players. There are numerous questions a coach might ask himself, such as the following:

Are the players having fun? Are they active? What is the level of involvement – are all involved? Are the players co-operating,

sharing and helping each other?
Are the players considerate to each other?
Is the level of skill challenging enough to keep the game going?
Is boredom creeping in?
Is decision-making shared?
Are the activities achieving the planned objectives?
Have I planned and prepared considering the needs and characteristics of young players?

The coach needs to evaluate each session carefully, asking some of these questions along with positive reference to long-term aims and shorter-term objectives, so he can then plan the next session accordingly, ensuring progression and development.

The coach should also identify talent and where appropriate extend players' learning further by encouraging them to play in other groups, e.g. school → club; club → county → regional, etc.

PART 3
THE SUPPORT SYSTEMS

14
PRACTICE ROUTINES

This chapter focuses on a number of practice routines for areas of work. The objectives are:

1.   To give ideas as to the kind of practices that can be set up with players.
2.   To provide a starting point for coaches to use the knowledge of progressive practices to consider the progressions.
3.   To stimulate coaches into modifying the ideas to suit their own needs.

The areas covered are running with the ball and passing; running with the ball and scanning; passing and receiving; passing and moving into space; intercepting; goal-scoring; centring; tackling, closing down, channelling; small sided game; and retaining possession.

There are examples of practices in other areas of work to which the same procedure can be applied.

Running with the Ball and Passing

PRACTICE 1
Objectives   Dribbling and passing.
Procedure   Two teams face one another at diagonally opposite corners of a rectangle 15m by 5m. A dribbles the ball along the side of the rectangle and passes to the leading player of team B on receiving a cue from B (verbal or visual). The pass cannot be made until A is beyond the corner cone. B then continues the exercise and A joins the other group.
Variations   Forehand stick dribble; Indian dribble; or reversing the circulation to organize left to right passes. Adjusting the point of the pass.

PRACTICE 2
Objectives   Dribbling, beating a player and passing.
Procedure   As for practice 1, but each team is faced by two sets of cones each about 1–1.5m wide across their path along the long side of the rectangle. The first player A runs with the ball and uses left to right drag followed by right to left drag to beat the wall of cones (1–1.5m wide). At the end of the run A passes to B at the front of the other team on receiving cue from B.
Variation   Having a wall pass with a stationary player between the two walls.

PRACTICE 3
Objectives   Dribbling and passing at speed.
Procedure   A line of six cones 4m apart is laid out. Two players about 5m apart, one on either side of the line, dribble and pass the ball without hitting the cones. A target (stick) should be shown for the passer. The ball is passed to the next pair at the end of the run and they continue the exercise.
Variations   Particular passes; or distancing the players or cones apart.

Running with the Ball and Scanning

While all exercises where players run with the ball and either pass or avoid obstacles involve scanning, it is useful to have a few that are used to emphasize this vital part of a player's skill repertoire.

PRACTICE 1
Objectives   Dribbling and scanning.
Procedure   The group are in a confined area, each player with a ball. They have free

choice to dribble wherever they wish. Avoiding others should be emphasized.

PRACTICE 2
Objectives Dribbling, scanning and passing.
Procedure Over a distance of about 25m a wide variety of cone patterns can be developed to challenge players.
Common faults Moving too fast to perform the skills; ball too close to the feet.

PRACTICE 3
Objectives Dribbling and scanning.
Procedure Two players face each other about 10m apart with a wall of cones 1–1.5m wide between them. The two players dribble toward one another at the same time and beat the wall of cones using the same method. As they become more skilful at scanning, the wall can be removed and they time their movement in relation to each other.

PRACTICE 4
Objectives To develop scanning, eye-to-eye contact and passing.
Procedure Players dribble the ball in a confined area. If they can establish eye-to-eye contact with the colleague, they exchange balls with a pass.

Receiving and Passing

The following practices are only a few of the very many that can be created to develop these skills. This basic format can be modified for all the types of passing and receiving players may need to practise.

PRACTICE 1
Objectives To develop the ability to control the ball and prepare for a subsequent skill under increasing pressure.
Procedure A player receives a pass from a colleague and as he controls the pass he manipulates the ball so that he can move off in any chosen direction.
Variations Altering the angle of pass and the types of control (body and foot position)

to emphasize particular areas of the pitch, e.g. left wing.

PRACTICE 2
Objective To provide concentrated practice for control and passing.
Procedure A is the target for all passes from B, C and D. B passes to A who passes to D; C passes to A who passes to B; and D passes to A who passes to C.
Variation Every time a player receives the ball, he dribbles it around the cone which is 2–3m behind him.

Passing

PRACTICE 1 Fig 173
Objective To promote the quality of passing to a colleague.
Procedure Using an area about 15–20m^2 A passes to B and then moves to receive a pass. A begins the process again with B and then with C until A has completed the square. B and C concentrate on the quality of the passing. D can begin diagonally opposite A and begin at the same time.

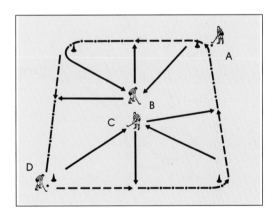

Fig 173   Practice 1.

Variations Reversing the direction; increasing the speed; varying the type and direction of pass; or putting four passers in the centre.

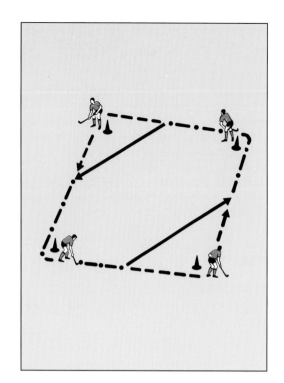

Fig 174   Practice 2.

PRACTICE 2 Fig 174
Objective   To develop the skill of passing on the run.
Variations   Reversing the direction or varying the type of pass.

Passing and Moving into Space

PRACTICE 1 Fig 175
Objectives   Passing to and running into space.

PRACTICE 2 Fig 176
Objective   To practise moving into space using square, through and back passing.

PRACTICE 3 Fig 177
Objective   As in Practice 2, but with a different pattern of running into space.

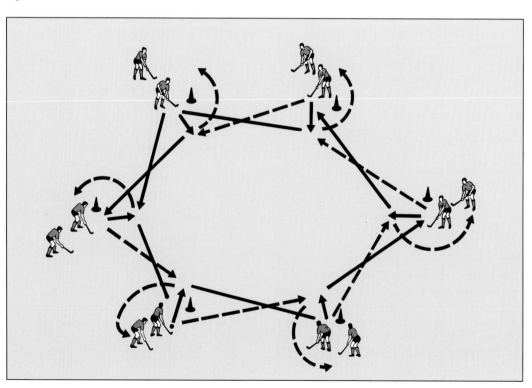

Fig 175   Practice 1.

198

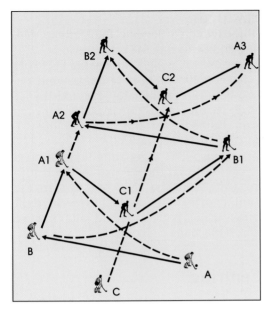

Fig 176(a)   Practice 2.

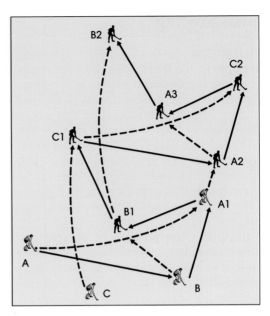

Fig 176(b)   Practice 2.

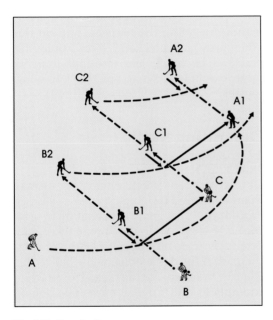

Fig 177   Practice 3.

PRACTICE 4 Fig 178
Objective   To practise a loop, through passing and moving into space.

Intercepting and Passing

PRACTICE 1
Objectives   To practise leaving a gap and intercepting the pass.

Procedure   In an area about 20 × 5m two players pass the ball along the ground from one end to the other. A third player attempts to intercept the pass on the forehand and reverse stick. The interceptor should experiment with: the size of gap that can be left and the interception still made; the distance from the striker; and how late the movement into the gap can be left.

PRACTICE 2
Objectives   To intercept a pass and make a pass to a colleague.

Procedure   As for practice 1 with the interceptor making a pass to another player after the interception.

Variation   Wider range of passes demanded; play 2 vs 1 with a colleague against the player who made the pass.

199

Goal Scoring

PRACTICE 1

Objective To emphasize the importance of controlling the ball well prior to shooting.

Procedure Six feeders each with two hockey balls are positioned in two arcs of three players 15–20m from the shooter who is at the top of the circle. The shooter has to control each pass near the top of the circle and make the strike at goal. Each feeder plays one ball in sequence until all twelve balls have been passed. The players then rotate.

Variations The position of shooter and feeders can alter; two extra attackers can be added to take any rebound shots from goalkeeper; or the shooter can be expected to move into space to collect the passes.

PRACTICE 2

Objective To combine dribbling, passing and shooting.

Procedure A line of cones is placed between the half-way and 25yd lines about 5m to the side of the centre of the pitch. The player dribbles through cones and plays a wall pass with a colleague near the top of the circle and shoots. A defender provides only moderate pressure on the shooter.

Variation The defender can increase the pressure on the attackers and the wall passer can choose to retain the ball and shoot.

PRACTICE 3

Objective To practise shooting from rebound situations.

Procedures A player shoots in front of goal into a barrier and a colleague takes the rebounds. After each rebound shot, the rebounder must move over to a group of balls a few metres in front of the post and score with one.

Variations A player passes the ball to the forehand stick of a colleague (5m from goalline) who lays it into space in front of the goal. The first player follows the pass to take a snap shot at goal. The goalkeeper can vary the amount of pressure put on the attacker.

PRACTICE 4

Objectives To develop the skills of passing and deflecting the ball at goal.

Procedure A winger strikes the ball from a position 10m from base line toward the area between the penalty spot and the far post. At the same time a colleague runs from the edge of the circle in the CF position to deflect the ball.

Variations The wing runs with the ball before centring; the CF passes the ball to the wing from the 25yd line to start the routine; or passing the ball from the right wing, using both forehand and reverse stick deflections.

Centring

PRACTICE 1 Figs 178 and 179

Objectives To practise the direction and timing of a variety of centres.

Variations In Figs 178 and 179 how could extra pressure be put on the right wing without negating the practice, and on the other principal attackers? How could the practices be made less stressful than in these examples? What are the left wing centres?

Defending Skills

PRACTICE 1

Objectives To practise closing down, channelling and tackling.

Procedure This game is played in an area 5m wide and 10m long. The attacker and defender start at opposite ends of this channel. A third player feeds the ball to the attacker from outside the area. The attacker attempts to beat the defender. The defender cannot move from the baseline until the ball is passed and aims to close in on the attacker, channel and tackle. If the attacker has not beaten the defender within 5–7 seconds then the defender has won, as that is sufficient delay in a game situation.

Variations Altering the type of pass and the position of the feeder. How does this alter the challenge for the defender?

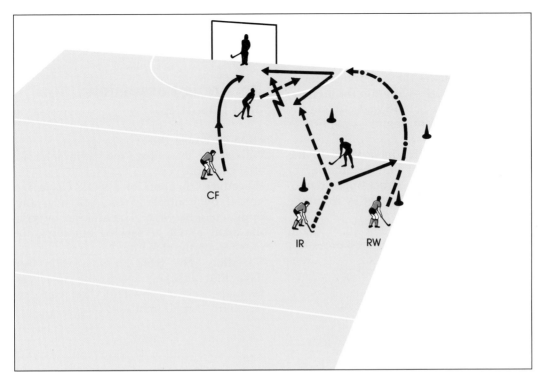

Fig 178   Practice 1.

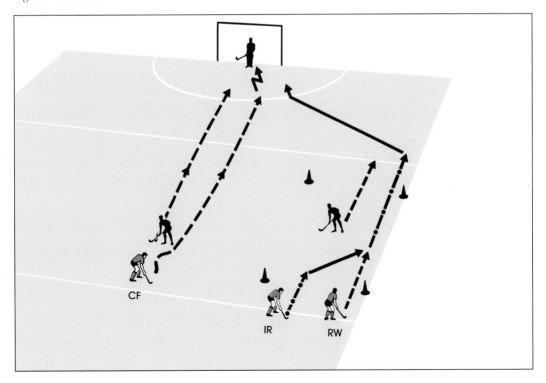

Fig 179   Practice 1.

PRACTICE 2 Fig 180

Objective To develop the skill of tackling in retreat.

Procedure A takes the ball and attempts to get a shot at goal having run through the zone. B starts 1m behind and outside the area. The movement begins as soon as A starts.

Variations The defender begins on the left and this time level with the attacker; or he begins closer to the goal but wider so that the covering movement is from the side.

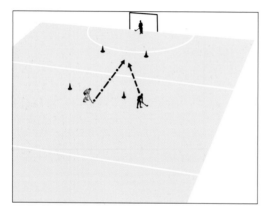

Fig 180   Practice 2.

PRACTICE 3

Objective Group defending against attack.
Procedure Three defenders plus a goal-keeper play against four attackers. The attackers start with the ball on the half-way line. The defenders must be outside the 25yd line at the start. The attacking four have 15 seconds to attack and create a shooting opportunity.

Variation Dictating defensive starting line-up (e.g. one defender at the top of the circle).

Retaining Possession and Passing

PRACTICE 1 Fig 181

Objective To utilize the extra man in attack to score.
Procedure A game of 3 vs 3. Goals are scored by controlling the ball over the opponent's baseline. The attacker outside the area cannot be tackled but can only move along the side line.
Variation The team in possession can have four attackers inside the area. On losing possession, the defending team can have only three defenders.

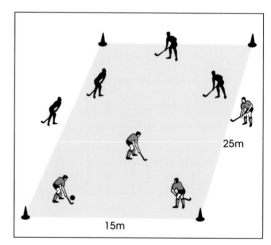

Fig 181   Practice 1.

202

15
PREPARING PLAYERS

Apart from promoting good relations with the players and developing their technical and strategic skills there are also the physiological and psychological spheres that the coach needs to consider.

It is not the purpose of this book to provide in-depth analysis of these spheres. There are many excellent texts on these and there are courses run by the National

Understanding Players
This is a key factor in all aspects of coaching, and the physical and mental preparation are no exception.

The basic factor that coaches must never forget is that players play hockey because they enjoy it. At the highest level the actual performing may not be a fun exercise, but if at the end it was a fulfilling experience then the enjoyment factor has been rewarded. Players will accept the rigours of training and practice if they see the work as worthwhile. If in the process they can also fulfil the enjoyment aspect then so much the better. While coaches should endeavour not to pander to the enjoyment factor at the expense of progress, they should nevertheless remember how powerful a motivator it is.

Involving players in the goal setting of as many aspects of the coaching as possible generates greater interest in and commitment to the objectives. The achievement of these then satisfies the enjoyment factor. The philosophy of working 'with' the players, therefore, promotes the process that recognizes and uses the importance of self-motivation. This crucial factor is borne out of a positive attitude toward the objectives, and most positive attitudes are based upon the good feelings gained from performance (i.e. enjoyment).

Fig 182   Debbie Bowman of Australia in the 1988 Olympic Games.

Coaching Foundation (NCF) for coaches. However, this chapter offers guidelines to the physiological and psychological preparation of players at club and international level.

Physiological Preparation

Hockey, particularly now that so much is played on artificial turf, demands a good foundation of aerobic fitness although it is also a multiple sprint activity. This latter characteristic is in reality a whole series of short bursts of activity of varying intensity over a variety of distances. There is, therefore, a considerable demand upon the player to work anaerobically and recover during periods of comparatively low-level activity. These characteristics need to be reflected in the physical preparation programme.

203

Aerobic Training

Aerobic means using oxygen and so this area is concerned with the process of getting oxygen to the working muscles during the game and consists of the lungs, heart, blood vessels and blood. Aerobic training improves the efficiency of this system, so that blood laden with oxygen can be distributed more easily to the muscles at any given workload and waste products, such as lactic acid, can be removed more easily. A subsequent result of training is that more work can be done by the player and the recovery rate is improved so that less rest is required between working periods.

For pure aerobic training, running at relatively low speeds for reasonably long distances (6km) or periods of time (30 minutes) is sufficient, but because the game of hockey is unlike this it may be advantageous to shorten the distance (e.g. 4km) and increase the speed. This will introduce an anaerobic aspect into the training, but it will be a beneficial one.

It is also possible to develop the aerobic system by running even shorter distances through repetition work. To make this effective the running time, excluding the resting phases, ought to be at least 15 minutes. Continuous relays around an interesting circuit can be an excellent method of group training. Each leg of this continuous relay ought to be of different lengths to add to the interest. While this will not be pure aerobic training, it is ideally suited to the nature of the game and will produce the desired results if done properly.

Fartlek running can be used individually or as a group. This is running at a varied pace and is similar to the continuous relay, except that the resting phase demands activity (walk or jog). If it is important that even this training is game-related to maintain the interest of the players, then perhaps the hockey run or a variation on it would be a useful exercise (Fig 183).

A good test of aerobic stamina is a 12-minute run measuring the distance covered or, if that is not feasible, then running a set distance (e.g. 3km) and measuring the

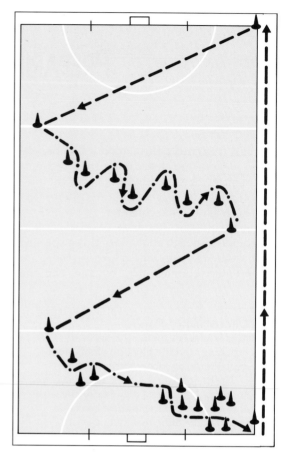

Fig 183 The hockey run is a useful exercise to improve aerobic stamina.

time taken. There is also an excellent multi-stage fitness test available from the NCF. These simple processes can provide excellent feedback and motivation to players during a training programme.

Anaerobic Training

Anaerobic means working without oxygen and this occurs when you demand sudden bursts of energy from your body. The aerobic system can keep you working at a low level of output for long periods, but you can increase the output beyond the capacity of the aerobic system only by using the anaerobic system. This system, however, is split into two parts: the alactic (or phosphocreatine) energy system and the lactic energy system.

Fig 184   Richard Charlesworth attempts a diving tackle as Volter Fried breaks through for West Germany against Australia in the 1986 World Cup.

THE ALACTIC ENERGY SYSTEM

This is able to provide a great deal of energy but is depleted rather rapidly (up to 15–20 seconds of sub-maximal anaerobic activity). However, the replenishment of this energy source is also rapid and it is probable that much of the energy for the bursts of activity in hockey come from this system. Ideally, training should be at maximum effort for between 5 and 20 seconds and with a rest to work ratio of 5:1, with the resting periods being gently active. This is the training that promotes acceleration and speed. While it can be done without stick and ball, it is particularly beneficial to develop these qualities allied to the skills of the game. The ability to accelerate and run at speed with the ball are great advantages on artificial turf. Many routines can be set up to marry the physical training with the skills and this method will satisfy the enjoyment factor in players. For club players this is essential to maintain enthusiasm.

THE LACTIC ENERGY SYSTEM

This has the advantage of producing high power output from the muscle for 30–40 seconds. Unfortunately, the body does not let you have something for nothing and the 'cost' of this output is that lactic acid accumulates in the muscle and has to be cleared by the blood (some is neutralized in the blood while the organs such as the kidneys and liver also help out). At the end of strenuous exercise it is advisable to keep moving so that the blood flow to muscles is maintained in order to clear accumulations of lactic acid (hence the 'warm down'). Training for this system should be done at no less than 90 per cent of maximum effort and the work intervals ought to be between 30 and 40 seconds with a rest to work ratio of 3:1. Players should not be asked to do more than six repetitions before a longer rest of 8–10 minutes is given.

It is this type of training that develops the ability of players to continually produce bursts of high-level activity. Not only is the quality of the performance promoted but also the ability to recover more rapidly during the period of resting or low-level activity is enhanced. This development provides the player with the opportunity to be able to reproduce periods of high-level activity throughout the game.

Training for the lactic energy system is particularly demanding and while elite players are able to cope psychologically with a purely physical training session emphasizing anaerobic stamina, it is better to modify a programme for club players to use stick and ball exercises as the vehicle. Experience shows that this interests the club player and the work rate and concentration are high.

There are many skill exercises that can be modified to produce an anaerobic training effect. If the exercises are performed in groups of four with one working at a time, then the rest to work ratio of 3:1 is achieved. Training exercises could be structured to include the following skills:

1. Passing and controlling.
2. Running, controlling and passing.
3. Dribbling and passing.
4. Running and shooting.
5. Dribbling and shooting.
6. Defending skills.

It is recommended that junior players are given their own programmes emphasizing skills and strategies, rather than the physiological training.

Training Programme

At club level it is probably better to have the same programme for all players.

Aerobic training needs to take place during the two or three months preceding the start of the season, with anaerobic training being used as the ongoing weekly diet during the season.

This pattern allows the inclusion of skills work during the season when it is most needed. If players are expected to train on their own, in addition to the weekly group

---

Mobility Exercises

Mobilizing is an important aspect of preparing for strenuous activity (match or training session). This is not only because an improved range of movement in a muscle group may over a period of time help enhance performance but also, and much more important in the short term, it specifically prepares the muscles for the subsequent work by raising their temperature and increasing the blood and oxygen supply.

Exercises for stretching are innumerable but they should cover the major muscle groups and joints (neck, back, hamstrings, gastrocnemius, Achilles tendon, chest, hips, groin, spine, quadriceps, shoulders, abdominals, and so on). These exercises should be done without jerking or bobbing. They are usually included in a warm-up before a game or practice session (10 minutes of stretching is the minimum) but other exercises, such as short explosive activities on the major muscle group and performing the skills required in the sport itself, should also be included.

At the end of all training sessions and matches the warming down should include low-intensity running and stretching exercises. This process has a very beneficial effect on the body's ability to prepare for subsequent sessions of activity.

---

training, then the following points are important to consider:

1. Heavy training sessions should occur early in the week.
2. Players should not train heavily the day before an important match.
3. If matches cut into the training programme (e.g. midweek) then a short intensive session should be done after the midweek match.
4. Speedwork should be done later in the week.

At the elite level the training programmes can be designed with a clear objective: to peak physically at a particular time, perhaps

Exercise	Repetitions	Intensity/Speed	Rest/Recovery
3 miles	1	21 minutes	
4 miles	1	28 minutes	
800m	6	3 minutes	3-minute jog
600m	8	2 minutes	2-minute jog

six to eight months ahead. Within these programmes there are training cycles that are followed by all, but the specific work is orientated to the individual with reference to his present state of fitness; the time necessary to reach his desired fitness peak; his lifestyle (business, hockey and social commitments) and his age.

The following gives an outline of the types of training and the training cycles used within the preparation of the Great Britain Olympic Men's Team in 1988.

AEROBIC TRAINING
Aerobic exercise does not have to be done at maximum in order to have the maximum training effect.

Type of training   Continuous running or interval running.
Distance to run   4,800m is a minimum.
Duration of work   In *continuous running* the duration should be at least 20 minutes. In *interval running* the duration (excluding rests) should be at least 15 minutes.
Speed of running   The examples in the table above give an indication of the speed of running initially but obviously players should seek to improve it.

As you progress, you should increase the speed if aerobic training is to continue efficiently. Accuracy in times for interval running (e.g. 800m, 600m) will be gained from the following method:

1. The player must time himself over 1,600m as fast as possible.
2. The time must be divided by four.
3. The target time for each 400m now is that time plus 3–4 seconds.
4. The targets for each 600m or 800m can similarly be established.

5. The rest period should equal the work period.

ANAEROBIC STAMINA
Anaerobic sessions are bound to be hard work and *must* be done properly. They may include:

Fartlek running   This is the constant repetition of walk-jog-sprint pattern over set distances (30–50m normally for games players) for a predetermined period of time (15–35 minutes). The pattern must be kept constant but you could vary the distances and the time could be altered or spaced, e.g. 10 minutes work; 5 minutes skills/rest and repeat three times.

With a little imagination the hockey pitch can be used as the basis of players' fartlek running, introducing stick and ball also.
Interval running   90 per cent maximum pace:
   2 × 400m (2 minutes rest) or 3 × 400m
   3 × 150m (walk back) or 4 × 150m
   4 × 100m (walk back) or 4 × 100m
Stick and ball work   This is the most difficult work to do and maintain a training effect. It is *vital* that you maintain repetitive high-quality work in order to build up oxygen debt, lactic acid in the system. Any repetitive practice with about six balls will suffice but players must make certain that the distances they run, the pace they work at and the intervals of rest ensure that their body is under anaerobic stress. They should work for 20–30 seconds at 90 per cent maximum with a resting period of 1 minute, reducing it down to 35 seconds.
Hill runs   Sprinting up the slope (15–20 seconds work) with 2–3 minutes rest. This should be repeated six to eight times.
Speed work   Short distances (10–50m), maximum output, work:rest ratio 1:5. Stick

207

and ball should be used if possible and 750–1,000m covered per session.

In order to give players every chance of training really effectively they must make certain that they warm up and cool down properly and that their diet is good (replenishing glycogen stores and having a good protein intake). To put the emphasis upon power, the distances on the interval running must be reduced and the fartlek runs cut out.

STRENGTH TRAINING
This can be done by using body weight exercises, small dumb-bells, etc. and multi-gym equipment.

The emphasis in all these methods should be to use sub-maximal weight and do the exercises quickly so as to build up the fast twitch fibres (particularly in work on the legs). It is essential that exercises cover the major muscle groups of the arms, shoulders, trunk and legs.

The weight-training session should include eight to ten exercises as a minimum. Each exercise should be repeated eight to ten times; this is one *set* of exercises. Players should do three sets on each exercise, with a short rest between each set before moving on to the next exercise. A good guideline for the weight to use is two-thirds of the maximum a player can lift in that exercise. Heavy weights should *not* be used when working on hamstrings and muscles of the trunk (abdominal and back).

AGILITY WORK
This includes skipping, triple jumping pattern (off either foot), bounding and running up steps and improves balance, footwork and leg power.

REMEDIAL WORK
This is the area in the physiological preparation of players that needs attention early in the programme so that it can be maximized by the tournament. The players themselves can usually identify the area they wish to improve most without the coach telling them!

Training Cycles

The training cycles followed in the Olympic programme are shown in the table opposite. Only the final twenty weeks of the programme are shown. Prior to this there had been the final preparation for a tournament in April and before December 1987 the principal training was aerobic work.

During the final twenty week programme there were two monitoring sessions in the Olympic Medical Centre at Northwick Park Hospital. These sessions were important in that the physiologists were able to discuss the results with the player and modify the training programmes where necessary.

Since 1988 Great Britain have had the services of a consultant physiologist and a portion of the recent training programmes are shown in the table on page 210. These are only illustrations of the kind of work international players follow. They should not be followed or adopted without the advice of a physiologist or experienced coach.

Psychological Preparation

Team coaches have to understand their players if they are to get the very best out of them. Understanding them is very much about getting to know what they like and dislike about the sport, what motivates them to perform, their attitudes and values and many other things that are part of a person's personality. All this inevitably means that coaches are deeply involved in the psychological preparation of their players. This should not be threatening to coaches as much of it is common sense and may well be followed already. Coaches do not now need a whole new sphere of knowledge, but it will certainly help to learn about mental preparation for sport.

Sports psychology is certainly helpful in preparing elite players for top competition where every percentage point counts, but below this level its principal use is more as part of an education for young players.

The mind is not only a powerful part of

Week	Month	Tournament	Cycle	Training
20	May 1–7			Development of anaerobic stamina: 1. Strength work. 2. Skills training. 3. Some speed and agility work. 4. Personal remedial work.
19	8–14			
18	15–21			
17	22–28		1	
16	29–(4)	Malaysia Tournament		
15	June 5–11			
14	12–18			Anaerobic work with emphasis upon power and recovery: 1. Increasing stick and ball work. 2. Strength work (reduced). 3. Agility work.
13	19–25			
12	26–(2)		2	
11	July 3–9			
10	10–16			
9	17–23			Anaerobic work with emphasis upon speed: Stick and ball work of high priority and within training exercises.
8	24–30		3	
7	August (31)–6			
6	7–13	Amsterdam Tournament		
5	14–20	Lada Tournament		As for cycle 3. Training pattern to mirror Olympic playing programme.
4	21–27		4	
3	28–(3)			
2	September 4–10			Travel, acclimatization and final preparation.
1	11–17	Olympics	5	
	18–24	Olympics		
	25–(1)	Olympics		

GREAT BRITAIN SNR PROGRAMME
August–November 1990

	Weeks		Days	Runs	Days	Wts/Circuit
E N D U R A N C E	1	July 30	1	Hills I	2*	Weights I 15min jog
	2		3	Fartlek 20min		
	3		5*	Hills I 25mins fartlek	4	Weights III
	[*Remedial session]					
P O W E R I	4	Aug 20	1	Shuttle E/ Bounding 10min	2*	Weights IV/ 15min jog
	5		3	Shuttle D/ Hills III	4 / 4	Weights III/ circuit C
	6		5*	Hills II/15 min easy jog		
P O W E R II	7	Sept 10	1	1 mile (timed)/ Bounding 10min	2*	Weights II
	8					
	9		3	Skills/Shuttle A/ Bounding 15min	4	Weights III/ circuit C
			5/6*	Hills III/ Fartlek 25mins		
S P E E D I	10	Oct 1	1	1 mile timed/ Bounding 15min	1*	Weights III/ circuit C
	11					
	12		3	Skills/Shuttle A/ Bounding 20min		
			4	Hills III/ Shuttle F	5/6*	Skills/ Shuttle A
S P E E D II	13	Oct 22	1	1 mile timed/Skills/Bounding 20min		
	14		3	Shuttle A/Shuttle F		
	15		5	Skills/Bounding 20min		

top performance but is probably the key to the highest level of achievement. If a programme can help young players cope with the stresses of competition and use them positively then the potential of those performers will increase considerably. While a coach, of course, needs to understand the psyche of his players in every part of his work, there are some aspects of the interaction that demand greater awareness of the psychology.

When working with a player individually, it is important to understand how much personal input he wishes to give in terms of planning his programme, developing his game and discussing strategies. Some players want to give their views, others are more reluctant, while a few still want to be told what to do. During the final team talk before a game, one player may require firm direction as to the role to be played, whereas another prefers to verbalize the requirement calmly and quietly. All require the comments to be positive. Players have the opportunity before the game to view the opposition and the key areas of play and the coach can make use of their ability to see the game from a wider perspective than just their own role. It may be necessary to draw a viewpoint from some players (e.g. possible substitutes) to increase their involvement and even limit some players' desired inputs, as they could confuse matters.

Throughout these complex interactions one of the key factors is motivating players to give their very best performance. This can be done only if the coach is clearly aware of their motivational needs.

Over and above the individual psyche is the group psyche. This also has to be promoted, in order to develop 'team spirit'. This is done over time through both good and bad experiences, which will pull the team together promoting trust in one another. While the coach can be part of this, players are on their own on the field and must therefore be able to cope without the coach.

Recognizing the group psyche is also important when planning team talks. Prior to the Olympic final all had been said before and the 'feeling' within the squad that no one was going to stop them was such that gentle reminders were all that was necessary. The only time during the match when the coach has a real input is at half-time. Again the time is precious, so words must be used sparingly but wisely, making certain it is what the *players* need to hear. For example, a few questions/comments to all individually or to a group and then about three general points at the end can be made. Too many points to the whole group results in non-retention and lack of focus.

The best teams are those that while accepting and valuing the success they have, are always striving to improve. The quality of these teams is a result of the interaction between the members and their leader.

Match Preparation

The final phase of match preparation varies in length from a few hours to perhaps one and a half days, depending upon the type of competition. The role of the team management during this phase is to provide the players with every opportunity to perform to their maximum. This may include consideration of diet, medical treatment and rest periods, as well as the tactical and psychological preparation. This book deals only with the last two aspects which form the central part of the coach's work during this phase.

The tactical plan is simply the strategies that are going to be employed to try and gain ascendency over the opposition. Also, it will be necessary to consider when, where and by whom these strategies are to be implemented. These questions in turn demand a recognition of phases of play in the game and how to react to various situations (e.g. going one goal down; the opponents having a player suspended, etc.).

The psychological preparation is tied in very closely with the tactical preparation but the crucial factor is to assist the players in gaining a clear focus of their role both as an individual player and a team member. In

211

most cases these two areas of preparation are promoted by means of meetings.

Team meetings can be structured in many ways and, if used cleverly, can greatly motivate the team.

These meetings do not have to include everyone provided the objectives are commensurate with this structure.

For example, strategies at defending penalty corners do not necessarily require the attention of the whole team. These smaller meetings are advantageous in promoting discussions, but it is essential that the decisions are then conveyed to the whole team or squad. At the start of the final preparation before a game, it is useful to have a meeting in which the players contribute more than the coach. The objective of the meeting will be to gain the players' views of the approaching game. This process has a number of advantages:

1. The views and experiences of players are seen to be valued.
2. Players gain knowledge from one another.
3. Most players are positive and this promotes confidence.
4. It encourages players to watch matches more carefully when their opponents are playing.

Managing this type of meeting demands care and attention by the coach or manager. Experience suggests that the best results occur when all players are encouraged to contribute; the principal areas of discussion are led by the management; the management ask 'open' rather than 'closed' questions; and there is a nucleus of experienced players who can be used as catalysts.

Characteristics of the Best Team Meetings
1. Objectives are clearly identifiable.
2. The opportunity for dialogue rather than monologue exists.
3. All relevant parties are heard.
4. Clear conclusions and/or actions are determined.

These meetings can also be used at club level to decide the tactical plan for the forthcoming game at the weekend. Meetings would then probably occur prior to the final practice session during the week.

The most common team meetings occur within two hours of the match. All too often the management team tries to squeeze too much information and motivation into these meetings when the players really need clarity above all else. The objectives of this final meeting are to clarify individual and group roles; to confirm tactical plans; and to unify and motivate the team.

There are as many ways to structure and run these team meetings as there are coaches and managers, so it is impossible to provide a meeting that will be ideal for every player. The style and content will also be influenced by many factors.

Common Factors of the Most Effective Pre-Match Meetings
1. Positively structured comments that promote confidence.
2. Emphasis upon how the opposition will have to adapt to the team's strategies rather than vice versa.
3. Talks that start with the individual's contribution and then move to their team responsibilities.
4. Emphasis upon the core of their role followed by the extras they may offer the team.
5. Promoting strengths before any potential weaknesses.
6. Utilizing players to state or reinforce key messages.

There is no perfect time for a team meeting but it should be sufficiently close to the game so that the players will be able to retain their focus in the match situation and still have enough time for thoughtful preparation. If most players like to have 40 minutes prior to the match to warm up thoroughly, then the final meeting might be between one and two hours before the start. If this pre-match meeting has to be more detailed because of the lack of opportunity before the match day, then it should be earlier than two hours before the push back.

After the final meeting coaches are often in a difficult situation. Inevitably, they feel nervous because they have already played the game mentally and there is a desire to continually reinforce points to players. It is at this time that the coach can do his greatest damage to a player's preparation. He should carefully choose any words he uses and to whom he says them, suppressing any needs to express his own hopes, desires, fears and frustrations, etc. In addition, it is a time when it is appropriate for the captain to take a stronger lead, for it is to this person that the players respond during the match. It is up to the team, led by the coach's representative (the captain) to take responsibility for their own performance. The best service the coach can provide is to watch calmly so that at his next opportunity (half-time) he can provide valid and valuable input.

Half-time meetings are notoriously poor with too much emphasis placed on the first half and too many points made for people to assimilate properly. There are also other things going on e.g. drinks, kit repairs, treatment, etc.

The following general points may be helpful:

1. Having a system so that everyone will be ready for any group talk at roughly the same time.
2. Speaking individually to all the players considered necessary early in the half-time.
3. Making only two or three points to the group as a whole, as more than this is unlikely to be absorbed.
4. Focusing on what the players are going to do, not on what has happened.

At the end of matches coaches often desire to rapidly debrief or perform a post-mortem of the game! This should be resisted, so that everyone can have a more objective perspective on the performance. The situation may not allow too much quiet reflection, but regrouping between one and two hours after the game could provide more constructive evaluation and promote future performance improvement rather than immediate post-match judgements.

Team meetings are crucial to team development but to gain maximum return for everyone involved, they require just as much thought as any other area of player preparation.

16

TEAM MANAGEMENT

The objective of this chapter is to give an insight into the structure and idea of team management at international level. This information can then be used to help prioritize the support that can be given to a team and to define the order of that team management.

The team management is the principal support system for any team and it works to provide the players with every opportunity to perform to their potential in the competitive situation. The management may be a large team with specialized roles, or a smaller team with clear responsibilities to act as the link between the players and particular specialist requirements. This chapter focuses upon experiences of the international arena to identify and outline the various orders within team management. While many clubs and representative teams will be unable to match the resources available to international teams, the understanding of the roles will illustrate the range of support services that can be used to help players.

At the outset it is important to state that in Britain, generally speaking, the team manager has an important and visible squad leadership role. He is thus the first appointment, and is intimately involved with appointing the coach, team doctor, physiotherapist and the assistant manager, and selecting the players. This is not the case in the team management of other countries where it does not matter which member has ultimate responsibility, provided that it is clearly defined and understood. It is far more important to establish and develop a management team that has the necessary skills and expertise along with a commitment to work in harmony for the benefit of the whole squad.

Objectives of the Management Team
The major objective of team management, and of the management team, is to create a working environment that will enable both coach and players to maximize their potential. This working environment is not easily defined, nor is it constant. It is unique to each squad of players as the combination of the players' individual characters inevitably modifies the environment. The England and Great Britain Squads since Seoul have changed in character as experienced, strong characters such as Ian Taylor, Paul Barber and Richard Dodds have retired. The working environment, too, has changed.

The working environment changes through time as a squad progresses from the 'preparation phase' to the 'performance phase'. The input and influence of the team manager and all the management team has to be reconciled to these changes.

The team manager has to develop a management team to assist in the major objective. In doing so he will attempt to engage the services of experts in the important areas of techniques and tactics, physiology, psychology and medical aspects. Through consultation and discussion with the experts in the management team (or gleaning advice from experts outside the management team), the team manager strives to make the decisions most appropriate to create the best working environment, thus giving leadership to the management team and players alike. Through consultation and discussion the manager strives to achieve leadership without ownership.

Members of the Management Team

The management team at senior international level will ideally be made up to cover the following roles, which are based upon those developed within the Great Britain and England management teams during the last decade: manager, assistant manager, coach, assistant coach(es), doctor, physiotherapist, video technician, physiologist, sports psychologist and chef or nutritionist.

Finance, of course, at the end of the day will determine exactly how many individuals will be able to attend training and tournaments. Consequently, the various functions may have to be performed by the personnel afforded and several functions will then be performed by each individual.

Team Manager

The team manager is appointed to take overall responsibility for the performance of the team and is involved in the selection of players and the appointment of the personnel within the management team. His responsibilities of organization and motivation are similar to those of a managing director or chief executive.

He uses his expertise and experience to make judicious appointments of individuals with talents appropriate to the roles required within the management team. He should not be afraid of seeking advice from his non-executive directors (senior members of his association) or indeed from any knowledgeable person he so chooses.

Once he has helped in the appointment of the other members of the management team he has to quickly establish good working practices and communications, i.e. a good working relationship that promotes the working environment conducive to maximizing performance. He does this by trusting the individual, appointed on the basis of his ability, to work well within agreed guidelines towards agreed and achievable goals. Decisions in any of the functional areas are made after consultation.

The team manager has to be aware of what is happening in all the various areas. It is essential that he is well informed if he is to make good decisions and be able to justify those decisions to the management team and players alike. In almost all circumstances, since the primary objective is to improve performance on the playing field, the coach will be completely involved with the manager in investigating problems and making decisions. However, circumstances will occasionally arise in which the manager has to make decisions independent of the coach – whether it be on finance, players' problems or even to give the coach the room to operate without pressure.

One of the key areas of team preparation for which the team manager assumes responsibility is player and team motivation match by match. There is no definitive method of doing this.

The precise role of the team manager will become more apparent as the other roles are examined.

Assistant Manager

The assistant manager provides active rather than moral support to the team manager, performing many practical aspects – air tickets, luggage, kit distribution and laundry, acquisition of essential supplies on tour – thus allowing the manager more time and energy to devote to leading the team.

If, by careful selection, the assistant manager is also an experienced, well qualified ex-player or coach, he can also contribute to discussions on selection, tactics, training and video analysis with the manager and coach.

Coach

With all the complexities of organizing the management support services to the team under the direct responsibility of the team manager, the coach, who needs to be aware of, interested in, and, in many cases, party to decisions, can concentrate on what he is appointed to do. He has to get things correct on the playing field.

Fig 185   Great Britain – Olympic champions in Seoul in 1988.

Ultimately, the coach has to have an ideal style of play toward which all his plans and practices are aimed. While coaches need to have this utopian vision they must also recognize that it rarely pertains. In order to work towards the ideal he has to get down to more mundane matters of developing individual skill levels, developing group play within the team, developing polished set pieces and generally educating and moulding players into a team.

The bottom line inevitably becomes the development of strategies to enable his team to cope with the phases during which the team is under pressure without conceding goals, and to exploit those phases which the team dominates. Crucial to both phases – apart from recognizing that they occur – is the winning and converting (or defending) of that vital set piece, the penalty corner.

The achievement of the coach's objectives have already been discussed in much detail.

Assistant Coach(es)

In order to promote 'management succession' it is important to involve as many developing coaches as possible in the preparation of an international team. Judicious invitations to perform specific coaching tasks and generally be part of the tournament preparations can help future coaches formulate their ideas and techniques. If funds allow such an assistant coach could also usefully act as video technician.

Doctor

The nature of the game of hockey – players running and turning at high speeds and propelling hard balls with sticks – does lend itself to a number of acute injuries. A doctor is therefore an important part of the management team.

The team doctor is responsible for the co-ordination of treatment for injured players and ensuring that the correct form of

216

treatment is initiated as soon as possible. Injured players also need to be supervised during their rehabilitation and team management have to be kept informed of their progress *vis-à-vis* team selection. In the absence of a trained coach in physical education or an expert physiologist, the doctor may be the adviser on effective training methods.

When a team tours abroad the doctor ensures that appropriate vaccinations and overseas travel advice are given, such as avoidance of jet lag, and gastro-enteric and environmental hazards. Similarly, in the present sporting climate the doctor is vital in educating players about drugs and in assuring the Sports Council that measures have been taken to prevent misuse of drugs. The doctor is also responsible for fluid provision and replacement and ensuring that the timing and types of meal are physiologically appropriate.

To have the 'right' team doctor is less a precise science and more often down to pure chance. He must, of course, have the appropriate qualifications combined with a knowledge and interest in the sport or in sport in general. In order to understand the idiosyncracies of hockey players it is useful to have a doctor who has played some form of competitive sport himself. Most of the doctor's work on a tour is of the general practitioner type. Ideally then, a good GP with an interest in and understanding of sport and sports medicine is the sort of doctor to seek.

While on tour the management team are often 'apart' from the players but the GP nature of the team doctor constantly brings him into contact with the players concerning medical matters. Without breaking any confidences with his patients the doctor can play a valuable role in keeping the team management abreast of the 'mood' of the players. Under the stress conditions of a World Cup or Olympic games this can be invaluable.

Physiotherapist

The physiotherapist is often regarded as the key person of the medical service side of team management, as he runs on to the playing field the most often to assess and treat injuries. It is he that produces the magic sponge or spray that miraculously enables the player to battle through. Often it is also the physiotherapist's knowledge and experience that decides that an injury will get worse if the player remains on the field. The physiotherapist is therefore most often seen in action assessing traumatic injuries on the pitch and thus also has a key role to play in treating these injuries after the match. Indeed repair and rehabilitation of injured players is vital.

Of equal importance is injury prevention through long-term player education in stretching to improve flexibility and suppleness. This reduces the incidence of muscle injury though, of course, it cannot reduce the knocks from ball or stick. In the short term, pre-match warm-up and post-match warm down are part of the physiotherapist's role.

If on tour without a doctor, the physiotherapist can be put into difficult medico-legal situations. Inevitably, players will seek medical advice from who they consider as the 'medical' person. In the case of abdominal pain or any other specific medical condition the physiotherapist simply does not have the medical qualifications or experience to deal with the problem. This is why the BOA advise strongly that a physiotherapist should be accompanied by a medical officer whenever the team travels abroad.

Team manager, coach, doctor and physiotherapist make up the essential minimum management team for an international team on tour or at tournaments abroad.

If finances are tight then a doctor can be omitted without trepidation in the safer areas of northern Europe but even in Europe problems can arise. If, however, funds allow, the performance of the management team can be much enhanced by the additional inclusion of one or more of the following personnel. But, more often than not, these roles have to be fulfilled by the management team to a greater or lesser extent.

Video Technician

The video technician videos his team's matches and the matches of opposition teams to allow detailed analysis of pattern of play, individual players and set pieces. At present only the Germans, Dutch and Australians regularly afford this means of teaching, but if one looks at their tournament track record in the 1980s, it proves to be a worthwhile teaching tool, despite its cost.

Physiologist

In the constant quest for players with the fitness not only to survive a tournament but also to be able at the end to dominate opponents, it is essential to keep in touch with the latest advances in bio-mechanics and sports physiology. Training methods have to change with the evidence of detailed research and, of course, in hockey in the last decade, with changes in the demands of the game.

The transition from grass to synthetic surfaces and the advances in technique and equipment have seen the physical demands of the game change rapidly over the last decade. The proliferation of competitive hockey both at domestic (National Hockey League) and international (champions, trophies, sponsored tournaments) levels has made it very important to consider 'phasing' of training and 'peaking' at the right time.

For the international teams this means the involvement of a sports physiologist, preferably from a hockey background to avoid mixing training techniques from other sports. Regular physiological monitoring in a laboratory or by field tests is necessary to glean information on which to base the design of training programmes. Such programmes can be designed for the individual as well as for midfielders, strikers and defenders.

For club teams it is very important to investigate carefully the physical preparation of the team to avoid the temptation to follow the old adage that more is better.

Sports Psychologist

There are doubtless many learned volumes available that explain in detail the rationale behind sports psychology as a branch of that least understood science. As far as hockey players and hockey teams are concerned, the role of the sports psychologist is relatively easily understood if it is viewed as follows. The sports psychologist helps the players (and team management) to develop ways of controlling the controllable factors within the preparations for tournaments or matches and during the stress of the tournament or match.

Given that a wide variety of factors that could influence the level of performance are out of the player's control, such as the umpire's decisions, the ability and tactics of the opposition, the weather, the crowd, etc. it is vital to maximize control of those factors that can be controlled. The player's ability to control his own reactions to pressure situations and concentrate in practices and in matches, and his levels of motivation and relaxation are all areas in which the sports psychologist can help.

The sports psychologist could be invited to work with the players during the preparation phase, in particular to introduce them to a variety of mental skills, such as goal setting, visualization and centring which, like stick and ball skills, need to be taught, learned and developed.

Goal setting, which is much used in business management training and development, helps to focus attention on both performance and general preparations for training sessions and matches by clearly stating achievable objectives.

Visualization or *mental imagery* helps with the acquisition of particular skills or the execution of particularly important routines, such as penalty strokes, penalty corner insertions, stops and strikes, by vividly imagining the execution of the skills repeatedly in a relaxed state. Goal kickers in

Rugby Union and high jumpers in track and field are but two examples where skills are enhanced by such preparation, and often these skills are rehearsed immediately before execution.

Centring involves a series of breathing exercises that help control levels of excitement after traumatic events. This, if successful, slows the heart beat and aids regaining composure and thus concentration. Immediately after the elation of scoring a goal or the despair of conceding one are two occasions when concentration can waiver.

Although the sports psychologist can help to educate players in these respects and could probably have a strong effect on players in pre-match team meetings, it is in the former role of helping players to control uncontrollable factors that he would be used with an international team at present.

It is still the responsibility of the team manager and coach to know their players and to motivate them to play to potential.

Nutritionist/Chef

When defining the final few per cent in team preparation to enhance team performance, the ultimate source of a player's energy – his food – is an area of interest. Both in the preparation and performance phases the diet can be controlled to enhance performance and pre-empt problems.

When players are training hard in preparation for a tournament it is vital not only that they eat enough to provide enough energy but also that they eat the right food to provide what the body needs. In this context the advice of a nutritionist, or at least the analysis of a player's standard diet by a nutritionist, may reveal the need for adjustments in diet. In these days of fast convenience foods, the packet snacks, the pot noodles and the burger and chips may not be the correct training diet.

Similarly, during a tournament particularly abroad and especially in areas where the water and general standards of hygiene are unusual, or the local cuisine is not suited to the majority taste, a chef has proved very useful. Both the MCC and

previous hockey tours to India and Pakistan have seen team performances much reduced by violent outbreaks of 'Delhi-belly', 'Lahore lament' and the 'Karachi'!

In 1989–1990 the England team were accompanied by a British Telecom International-sponsored chef, both on the exploratory tour to Lahore in December 1989 and to the World Cup itself in February 1990. The excellent work of John Booth and Brian Kraven respectively in either cooking or supervising the cooking of the food in a hygienic manner and to the players' taste resulted in almost no gastro-enteric problems at all! For the one-off major tournament (like England football under Bobby Robson in Albania) a chef is a wise investment but as routine he is the ultimate luxury.

The Balance Between Preparation and Performance

During the preparation phase that should properly be subdivided into 'Selection' and 'Team Development', the relative importance of some roles and aspects emphasized within roles differ from those in the performance phase. These are shown in the tables overleaf illustrating the need for the management team to have a range of skills to be applied appropriately.

The Continuum of Management Support (Country to Club)

With unlimited funding, as might have been available in Eastern bloc countries before 1990 or as might be envisaged available in the USA, all the roles discussed in this chapter would be fulfilled in an attempt to gain every last percentage performance.

In reality the management team varies in its content from country to country and down to club level. For example, in the 1990 World Cup held in Lahore, Pakistan, the top five teams had the management support teams as shown in the table on page 221.

Prior to Team Selection in the Preparation Phase

Team manager	Co-ordinating the selection process with selectors and coach.
Coach	General concepts, global strategies, individual skill enhancement.
Video	Training and match analysis, analysis of past performances of potential opponents.
Physiologist	Early training phases (strength endurance) testing, education.
Sports psychologist	Education of players in mental skills and goal setting.
Doctor	Getting to know players.
Physiotherapist	Constant attention to injury prevention and treatment.

After Team Selection in the Preparation Phase

Team manager	Planning with the coach the policy for the tournament.
Coach	Detailed planning of set pieces (penalty corners, long corners, 16yd hits, free hits), detailed rehearsal of open play strategies.
Video operator	Analysis of goalkeeping as part of defence of penalty corners, analysis of attack penalty corners, detailed analysis of known opponents.
Physiologist	Normal coincidence of selection with final phases of training, i.e. power and primarily speed work.
Sports psychologist	Pre-tour or tournament preparation of strategies to cope with all envisaged situations, e.g. travel, food, water, climate and boredom in hotels.

Performance Phase

Team manager	Organization, selection and player motivation.
Coach	Analysis of opponents, planning tactics match by match, planning in-tournament practices.
Video operator	Filming opponents within tournament and ensuing analysis. Filming own matches to assist in debriefing.
Physiologist	Unless funds permit, not involved except if tournament is on home territory. In such circumstances this provides vital time for analysis of demands of this ever changing game.
Sports psychologist	As above.
Doctor	GP or counselling role, diet, assessment of injury.
Physiotherapist	Daily stretching and mobilizing sessions, pre-match warm-up and post-match warm down. Vital treatment of traumatic injuries.

Most, but not all, Poundstretcher National League Clubs now have a coach and a team manager though in many cases the manager has an informed interest rather than expertise in the playing issues and is thus regarded as administrative only. Some of the more enlightened, better organized, better motivated (and more successful!) clubs have team manager, coach, trainer and physiotherapists for major matches.

Providing the administration of a club side is carried out by a 'manager', the captain or the club match secretary, the key personnel to get involved would be, in order of priority, a coach and a physiotherapist.

Team managers in professional football come and go regularly (except at Liverpool FC) in the quest for success and profit. In

Position	Country	Management Support Team
1st	Holland	Team manager, coach, doctor, physiotherapist and video operator.
2nd	Pakistan	Team manager, coach, doctor and physiotherapist.
3rd	Australia	Team manager, coach, doctor, physiotherapist, assistant coach and selector on tour (video operator).
4th	Germany	Team manager, coach, doctor and masseur, trainer and video operator.
5th	England	Team manager, coach, doctor, physiotherapist, assistant manager (video operator), chef

hockey, the ultimate amateur team sport, both club and country are fortunate to find volunteers for such an onerous, taxing, pressurized (yet enjoyable) task.

Consequently, team managers are rarely summarily sacked but more often decide that without the success they had hoped for it is less than rewarding to continue in the role. Too often then clubs and even the national team are left looking for individuals with the right combination of talent, experience and motivation to carry out the task fulfilled by that lone worker, who after ten or twenty years of loyal service as club secretary, calls it a day . . .

In today's increasingly competitive and commercial world it is vital for club and country to look carefully at its planning for management succession. The Great Britain Men's Hockey Board led by T.I. Morrison (Chairman) and R. Self (Team Manager) carefully nurtured Bernard Cotton 1984–88 as Assistant Manager to facilitate the continuity of leadership style when BJC took over as GB Manager in 1988. In 1990 potential international team managers such as Paul Barber were being nurtured within the role of Manager England 'B' or Assistant Manager of England for the 1991 European Cup.

How many clubs, happy to have a manager, are thinking to the future and planning the development of his successor?

Team management must continually ask itself and its governing bodies difficult and far-reaching questions. Only through continual evaluation and discussion will the management team be able to lead the performers along the challenging path towards high-level achievement. When a manager and coach stop questioning one another in an open, honest and constructive manner, then they should seriously consider their future, for it is likely that they have become too comfortable.

The whole philosophy behind this book is that people (players, management, support staff) should be involved in the development of the spheres of activity that directly affect them. The leadership demanded by this perspective is one in which questioning plays a crucial part. If this book has prompted the coach to question his role and how he performs it, then it will have achieved its principal objective.

INDEX